Not Just Yorkshire Pudding!

The Story of Yorkshire's Food and Drink

Dulcie Lewis

COUNTRYSIDE BOOKS
NEWBURY BERKSHIRE

C000177625

COUNTRYSIDE BOOKS
3 Catherine Road
Newbury, Berkshire

To view our complete range of books,
please visit us at
www.countrysidebooks.co.uk

ISBN 1 85306 995 7
EAN 978 1 85306 995 6

The front cover picture was taken by Ann Holubecki,
and shows the author in the Victorian kitchen at the
Yorkshire Dales Countryside Museum, Hawes.

Designed by Peter Davies, Nautilus Design

Produced through MRM Associates Ltd., Reading
Typeset by CJWT Solutions, Newton-le-Willows
Printed by Borcombe Printers plc, Romsey

CONTENTS

A TASTE OF THINGS TO COME

Fine words butter no parsnips.

My Yorkshire mother-in-law could take a potato, an onion, and a pig's trotter, make dinner for six and still have some left over. My darling mother from Middlesex, on the other hand, was of the 'If-you-can't-smell-burning-then-it's-salad-for-tea' school of cookery. I come somewhere in the middle. I can produce a pretty decent meal for ten but not without brutish effort and a need to spend the next day in a darkened room. My cooking is not effortless, nor do I look gorgeous while doing it. My credentials for writing this book are that after 37 years married to a Yorkshire man and raising a family I have, like most women of a 'certain age', done some cooking in my time.

This is not a cookery book, however, and I assume that anyone reading it has a working knowledge of shortcrust pastry. I have included some interesting old recipes to illustrate what was being eaten at a particular time in Yorkshire and by whom, though sadly the fundamental needs of life were not equally shared out. The gut-busting courses of local game enjoyed by the Yorkshire gentry contrasted with the monotonous 'oat cuisine' of the workhouse and prison. In between were the fat-laden meals of cream, cheese and butter eaten by some farmers, locally caught fresh fish for those on the Yorkshire coast and bread and dripping in the towns.

What I also discovered was that besides Yorkshire pudding, pig and pies there was much good food to be enjoyed. Baking was an art; hospitality and enormous teas were shared with friends and neighbours, and behind all this were countless Yorkshire women putting three or more meals on the table every day. So this book is a homage to them and their hard work; loosen your belt, tuck in and enjoy some Yorkshire food from the past.

Dulcie Lewis

YORKSHIRE FOLK AND THEIR FOOD

God bless us all, an' mak us able
T'a eat all t' food 'at's on this table.

No book about Yorkshire seems complete without one often-quoted piece of advice; so let me get it out of the way early on:

Hear all, see all, say nowt,
Eat all, sup all, pay nowt,
And, if ever tha does owt for nowt,
Allus do it far thisen.

Of course this is a Yorkshire *man* supposedly advising his *son*, and I have always imagined it said 'tongue in cheek'; otherwise it gives a very bleak view of a Yorkshire male. I have known some generous Yorkshire men; indeed, my husband, although having a certain reputation for 'carefulness', has never failed to provide for his family. So having considered the merit of such wisdom we should ignore it and move on, for this cannot be said to apply to Yorkshire *women*.

A married woman in the past may not have had money of her own, although a strong northern woman probably controlled the household purse, with working men handing over the weekly wage in return for some 'baccy' money. She did not have money to throw around, but her generosity was shown in other ways. The importance of a 'good table', with fresh home-baked food prepared in a clean kitchen, and an ever ready kettle on the hob over a good fire was an ideal to which many aspired. Sometimes life fell a bit short of this ideal and the late Dr Will Pickles, a country doctor in Wensleydale, when offered a cup of tea while visiting a patient would judge the cleanliness of the kitchen by the state of the doorstep and took a cup or not, accordingly.

Shortly before her 100th birthday in September 2005 Marie Hartley, the distinguished Yorkshire writer and artist, took the time to reply to an impertinent letter of mine asking about her early collaboration with Ella Pontefract. Their first book, *Swaledale*, was published in 1934, followed by many others on all aspects of life and history in Yorkshire. I was interested to know how two young women, strangers in the Dales, were treated. 'We were usually very well treated by local Dales people. We were at times someone new to talk to and invite into their houses. The 1930s were a very different period from nowadays, when newcomers are now very numerous. Many Dales folk invited us into their houses for a cup of tea.'

In earlier times writers and travellers recorded Yorkshire hospitality in what must have been a wild place to visit. In 1771 Arthur Young, a writer on agriculture, who later became Secretary of the Board of Agriculture, recorded, 'No set of people whatever can be more hospitable, or more desirous of obliging, than the farmers in the north of England – it is the land of hospitality.' Although some have not been so noted for generosity, as the old saying when inviting guests to tuck in goes to show: 'Reach to and mak' yourselves at home; I is, and I wish you all were.'

Yorkshire is a robust county, and the attitude to food and drink reflected this. There may have been too much pig, pudding and pie for our modern sensibilities and expanding waists, but it was honest food, even if some of it slowly killed you. A Yorkshire doctor giving a public lecture on why heart disease was so high in the Dales, met with outrage when he declared, 'Ther's ower much pig and pasty eaten in these parts.'

Families ate together and the meal was treated with respect. It had taken hard work and good money to either buy the food or grow it, kill it and finally cook it. There may have been little but you ate with gusto, even if it was porridge for the umpteenth time that week. There were towns where 'porridge and stop' was normal. You ate porridge followed by what little food remained in the house – and then you stopped until there was money to buy more.

Any leanings to food fads and fancies were quickly crushed, and it was unforgivable to leave food on the plate: waste was not tolerated. Invitations out to tea always involved consumption of the inevitable seed cake, a plain sponge with pungent carraway seeds sprinkled on top. Children disliked this cake but would not dare to leave any for fear of offending and getting a clip round the ear later from mother.

In the past a Yorkshire man wanted plain, substantial food on the table, and the Yorkshire woman did her best to respond. Young women were expected to be able to cook, having helped their mothers before they could read and write. Good recipes were passed round and noted in a 'commonplace book', along with medical remedies and family accounts. Some might own a fancy cookery and household management book; Mrs Beeton and her publisher husband were quick to spot a niche market. Women were keen to learn, as an 1897 advertisement for Advanced Cookery in the small community of Hawes showed: 'The classes will commence in a few weeks and a Teacher will attend from the Northallerton School of Cookery. Nearly 100 names have been given in. The charge of 6d for the course. Each week during the winter months'.

Anne Bell's baking day: gingerbread, rich scones, mince pies, ginger snaps, apple pie, ground rice slice, lemon sponge and parkin. A tip from Anne: if gingerbread is left for a couple of days it improves, becoming moist and gooey on top.

A girl had her first apron as a Christmas present when she was about nine years old. Cooking and housekeeping were accomplishments which men noted when eyeing up a future wife. It was all very well having beautiful eyes and a shapely figure but, if they could not get three meals at least on the table every day, they would be passed over for a plainer, more reliable model. Consider this 'Hearty Advice to Young Ladies' from the *Wensleydale Advertiser* in June 1847:

> 'The buxom, bright-eyed, rosy cheeked young lady who can darn a stocking, mend trousers, make her own frocks, command a regiment of pots and kettles, feed a pig, chop wood, milk cows &., &., and be a lady withal in 'company' is just the sort for me, and for any worthy man to marry. But you, ye pining, moping, lolling, screwed up, wasp waisted, music-murdering, novel-devouring daughters of fashion and idleness, you are no more fit for matrimony than a pullet is to look after a family of one thousand chickens. The truth is you want, generally speaking, more liberty and less fashionable restraint; more kitchen and less parlour; more leg exercise and less sofa; more pudding and less piano; more frankness and less mock modesty, more breakfast and less bustle. Loosen yourselves a little and become something as lovely and beautiful as the God of nature designed you to be.'

I wonder if he ever found a wife?

It was the woman at home who saw to it that whatever little food there might be was served in a manner that filled you up.

Times have moved on, but there is still a generation who remember what it was like to be, not exactly starving, but never quite full. Bread was a great 'filler' and a woman made her own bread, otherwise she was 'shiftless'. Great doorsteps of bread spread with dripping, treacle or jam, eaten with the meal, after the meal or just before going to bed, would fill you up nicely. Friends tell me that in the West Riding if you had a tin of fruit as a treat it was served with a plate of bread and butter. The same principle meant fish and chips in a café came with a plate of white bread and butter.

The perfect example of a great filler is the Yorkshire pudding. This is the epitome of Yorkshire cooking: plain ingredients combined with a certain skill to produce something deliciously complete. Sadly, there are many outside Yorkshire who are unable to achieve the Holy Grail of the perfect pudding.

Here's to Yorkshire, my lads,
The land of good cheer;
The home of the pudding
Well known far and near.
Wed a lass who can make one
Is the theme of my song;
But so long as she's Yorkshire
You cannot go wrong.

Yorkshire pudding was served at the start of a meal with the cry, 'Them as eats most pudding 'as most meat', a cunning ploy to stuff those likely to eat most of the meat. Served as soon as it is cooked, a good Yorkshire pudding could be a metaphor for Yorkshire people themselves: a crisp risen edge and a soft middle. Served with beef or onion gravy, nothing is more delicious and satisfying.

The making of a good Yorkshire pudding is an imprecise art. Those who are consistently successful are vague on details, and every family has its own 'sure-fire' way of cooking one. However, all are agreed that it must be cooked in a large rectangular tin which is never washed but just wiped clean. (This presupposes that you have managed a perfect pudding and it is not some soggy mess stuck to the bottom and sides.) The bigger the tin, the better; preferably, it should cover the bottom of the oven. My friend's late Yorkshire father always described the size of the family pudding as 'an acre of pudding'. Never use small round bun tins; these are the preserve of southerners, gastro pubs and frozen food suppliers.

I have thought long and hard about including a recipe for Yorkshire pudding here, but I am not going to fall into that trap. I can imagine, you the Reader, throwing the book down in disgust saying, 'You don't make it like that!' The ingredients are plain flour, an egg, milk, water, salt and dripping and nothing should be simpler, except ... many of us cannot achieve a decent Yorkshire pudding. Asking a Yorkshire woman how she does it only leads to conflicting advice. Some never measure their ingredients, others insist the mixture be made just after breakfast or an hour before cooking and rested in a cold place like a pantry or outdoors with a plate on top. Others use just milk, or milk and water, or even better a handful of snow, beat it hard/not too hard, with a fork/whisk/wooden/metal spoon, in front of an open window, standing on one leg ...

The versatility of the Yorkshire pudding is endless. Chopped onions were added to the mixture, or a sprinkling of sage for roast pork and a pinch of mint for lamb. On busy days you made a double amount of mixture and ate one half as a savoury before dinner and the rest as a pudding with anything sweet such as jam, treacle and sugar, or apple and currants.

Originally the Yorkshire pudding was baked in a large pan underneath the meat as it rotated in front of the fire, the meat juices dripping onto the batter as it cooked. It has always had a special place in Yorkshire hearts, stomachs and even literature. The *Yorkshire Observer* in 1918 likened a good Yorkshire pudding to poetry: '... but it's a bit like Yorksher puddin', is poitri,' ah sez. 'There's nowt nicer when it is nice, wi' a sup o' gooid beef gravy – an' when ah sez gravy ah mean gravy, not weshin' up wotter – but

Ann Holubecki churning cream to make butter at the Dales Countryside Museum, Hawes. Each farm had its own wooden stamp to mark the butter. The butter was weighed into pounds and a normal amount for the farmer's wife to make and sell was 30lbs each week.

ther's plenty 'at can't mak a Yorksher puddin' fit to eyt. They'll gi'e tha a gurt dollop o' clammy soggy stuff 'at looks an' tastes as mich like putty as owt, an wi' gurt lumps o' raw flahr i't middle; or happen it'll be same as a buffalo hide wi' black blisters all ower it. An it's t' same wi poitri.'

The Yorkshire pudding was only one of many Yorkshire dishes with rib-sticking qualities. A working man needed 5,000 calories a day if he was not to lose weight. On the farms they enjoyed savoury pudding, and one farmer's wife told me her husband would eat this every single day, if she let him. I feel quite confident sharing Elizabeth Bradley's recipe with you:

Savoury Pudding

2 thick slices of white bread that have been soaked in cold water
1 tablespoon of medium oatmeal
2 tablespoons of self raising flour
¼ lb of suet
2 teaspoons each of dried sage, thyme and marjoram
1 lb onions chopped and part boiled
2 beaten eggs
milk to mix
Grated lemon rind and salt and pepper to taste

Mix all together and bake in a moderate oven for 1 to 1½ hours, and then higher for the last few minutes to brown the top.

A visitor at a remote farm might be offered simple food of homemade bread, cheese, apple pie and some milk. Or there might be something more substantial, as this story, handed down in the Hopper family, of the great rice pudding illustrates:

Redvers Hopper was a well-known Dales auctioneer and valuer. As a young man in the early 1920s, he went with his father to value a farm in Nidderdale. There was the farmer, his wife, four strapping sons and two daughters. Hospitality dictated that Redvers and his father were invited to share the midday dinner with the family, and they sat down to an empty table – but not for long. A huge wash bowl, the sort once used in the bedroom, containing a great rice pudding made with currants and cream from their cows was placed on the table. Nothing else appeared so they made a start on this Goliath of puddings, with everyone round the table, heads down, eating heartily in silence. This was followed by a great Yorkshire pudding and vegetables, including another large bowl, this time with mounds of creamy mashed potatoes topped by thick slices of cooked ham and eggs. Finally, in case anyone was still a bit 'peckish', a dish of apple pie and tea in pint pots appeared. It is hard to imagine anyone able to do any work that afternoon but this was normal, and the family would eagerly anticipate a tea about 4 pm of homemade cake and biscuits.

Puddings, cakes and rich tarts made from curds, cream and currants were served with lashings of cream, for 'cream spoils nowt but your best blouse'. On farms, cream was used by the women for the additional chore of butter making. The milk was left to stand and the cream collected from the top over a few days. Churning the cream into butter was hard work but when it was sold at market it was often 'pin money' for the wife. Further back in time, buying butter at the market needed care, especially if it looked a bargain, as 'veneering' hogs' lard with a thin layer of butter on the outside was not unknown.

Other good eaters were the coal miners of South Yorkshire who, at one time, were better off than many other skilled workers. When their shifts finished they expected to return home for a proper meal of Yorkshire pudding and roast meat or rabbit stew with vegetables from their allotments. Compared with the poor old weavers of the 1800s they were living like lords.

The one day of the week when you did not expect to eat well whatever your circumstances was Monday, as that was washday. 'They that wash on Monday have all the week to dry.' So you ate whatever had been hastily prepared amidst the piles of washing: cold meat and left-overs and, if you were lucky, a hard boiled egg cooked in the hot water of the set-pot – if it cracked, your egg tasted of soapsuds.

Thursday was generally baking day in town and country alike, and it took all day, with the fire needing feeding with dry sticks to boost it every so often. Children returned from school to find mother in the kitchen flushed, exhausted and the table piled high with the day's cooking. What is all the more remarkable is that any

A re-creation of a Victorian kitchen, with a sugar loaf in the middle of the table. A piece of sugar was broken off the loaf and then cut into smaller pieces with sugar snips and pounded with a pestle and mortar until it resembled the granulated sugar of today. (By kind permission of the Dales Countryside Museum, Hawes)

decent food at all was produced in the old black leaded kitchen ranges. Not for our grandmothers the joy of knowing when an oven had reached 180 degrees centigrade/gas mark 4. With the fire stoked up you relied on experience, generally by waving your arm about inside the oven, to know when it was hot enough. Bread dough was mixed before breakfast and left to rise in front of the fire, and baking needing the hottest oven was done first. The sequence went something like this: bread, teacakes, scones, anything with pastry; then sponges, followed by fruit cakes, parkin, gingerbread, and finally as the oven was 'falling' a stew for dinner. Phew!

I was shown an old photograph of a Yorkshire wife in wrap-round pinny baking on the kitchen table, except she is not working directly on the table but on a Yorkshire baking board with drop-down sides. This meant that if the master returned and needed something to eat, the sides were folded up and the tray put to one side to continue later, thus causing no inconvenience to the master and his mealtime. Many men might wish to return to those days when their food requirements were paramount, although none now would dare use the old grace before mealtimes that went: 'Ere's tiv me an' mi wife's husband, not forgetting missen'.

Yorkshire women were never afraid of mass catering. Feasts and tea festivals, parish teas, harvest suppers and Sunday school outings, Friendly Society marches, gatherings – somewhere in the county there was a party. Sometimes drink was taken, unlike the teetotal Love Feasts, which brought together the local Methodist churches for an enormous picnic of bread, fruit, curd tarts and cake, with hymn singing, personal testimonials of faith and a good sermon. Brimham Rocks, the scene of many a Sunday school outing, provided a magnificent backdrop. In the 1770s we know that 1,500 Yorkshire Methodists gathered there for a Love Feast. It rained.

Love Feast Cake

2 lbs of flour
2 ozs baking powder
1 lb each of sugar and currants
5 ozs each of butter and lard
8 ozs of sultanas
peel of a lemon and spices
3 beaten eggs

Rub fat into flour and add the rest of the dry ingredients.
Add the eggs and mix to a firm dough.
Bake in a greased tin, in a moderate oven, until cooked.

The *Wensleydale Advertiser* reported in June 1847 on a Tea Festival and a dance at which there were 2,000 people, and what a good 'do' it must have been: 'At 4 o' clock Tea was served in the marquee on the Shawl – the repast, as on previous occasions, uniting lighter delicacies with substantial comforts. The ladies who presided at the tables were really indefatigable in their exertions to serve their guests who, in long succession, partook of the entertainment

A Women's Institute Group Produce Show in Wensleydale in the 1950s. These members were not afraid to cook. (Ann Holubecki Collection)

provided.' Ladies really knew how to be 'indefatigable' then; how many of us would do it now?

A more modest sort of party and one that was popular in country areas was a 'rugging' party, with a 'toffee joint' . This was not as law breaking as you might at first think: it was a party where you made rag rugs and toffee. 'The toffee was poured on to a slate slab, cut into strips and paper placed over it so that one could just see the ends. A participant made a choice, but as the toffee had been cut into various lengths a strong element of luck came into it. At one rugging night a wag placed a duck in the chimney. The duck descended and spoiled the toffee.' I suppose you had to be there.

There were some parties you had to miss. However, in Yorkshire, your 'passing on' was made easier knowing you were to be buried decently, with cold ham and tongue. Dales people desired a 'menseful' funeral; one undertaken with all the niceties observed. Families paid 'bidders' to visit the local community and invite people to the funeral. Funeral cakes, similar to shortbread, were made by the deceased's family, wrapped and sealed with black sealing wax and given to the waiting mourners. In the 1880s this refreshment was wrapped in paper printed with the deceased's name, date of death and a verse of grim comfort.

Only the poorest failed to give a funeral tea or dinner of roast meat with all the trimmings. A large gathering and more elaborate food indicated the status of the deceased. The funeral of Edward Watson of Coverdale was an expensive affair, with payments for 'the bidder', the coffin, shroud, vicar, sexton, tolling of the bells and liquor, as people arrived. Afterwards the mourners ate: '10 stone of beef, 92 lbs of mutton, a leg of veal, 1 guinea's worth of shortcakes, 2 cheeses and the family paid a woman for six days' work to get it all ready.'

You cannot blame today's women, juggling work and family life, for turning their backs on the life I have just described. Today's lifestyle, except perhaps in farming, does not require such time-consuming preparation of heroic meals. Family eating has changed with the microwave, separate meals and instant food, as has dining out. Yorkshire towns now have elegant bistros and restaurants; our pubs are gastro pubs, with reviews in glossy magazines. Close your eyes and you could be eating in Hampstead, Hereford or Harrogate. Yet, in the heartland of Yorkshire, there still remains an appreciation of simple food and drink taken in unpretentious surroundings. An elderly gentleman from my village who received an invitation to a wedding reception to be held in a be-swagged marquee at our local country house hotel remarked, 'I reckon nowt to eating in a tent.'

DINING IN STYLE

'I now felt haste for dinner... A Boiled Fowl, Cold Ham,
Yorkshire Pudding, Gooseberry Pye, Loyn of Mutton Rst.,
Cheesecakes. A better dinner, and better dress'd, I never sat
down to; but fear that the charge will be heavy, –
1s 6d, at least: We shall see.'

The Hon. John Byng, on visiting the White Swan
at Middleham in 1792

The old saying 'you get what you pay for' proved right in this instance. At the end of his three day stay, John Byng, later to become Viscount Torrington, received a bill for £1 0s 10d and was not happy. 'Aye, I was close in my guess, at their unconsciable charge.' So dining out was never cheap, and it is as well to know that a Yorkshire rural labourer in the late 1700s had a weekly wage of between 7s 6d and 9 shillings, depending on the season, a West Riding weaver 16 shillings, and a skilled Sheffield cutler 17s 6d.

Dining in style is difficult for us to define now. What was considered a fine meal in the 18th century would have us complaining to the head waiter and refusing to pay the bill. In order to travel successfully in the past you needed a strong constitution. Once the monasteries were destroyed, eating away from home became difficult and dangerous. If you were not set upon by cutthroats and footpads, the ale you drank contained unlikely ingredients, such as hens' droppings and ground human bones from the local charnel-house, to bring it up to strength.

A traveller might use one of these rough and ready ale houses, but it was often no more than the kitchen where the wife or out-of-work husband brewed their own ale, and very few offered a bed for the night. There were some inns on the major routes but otherwise you relied on the kindness of strangers to take you into their home. However, the rogues and vagabonds intent on taking

The 'civil' George Inn in Coney Street York, by Henry Cave, 1807. The building was demolished in 1868.

advantage of others on the roads did not make ideal house guests. Travelling further than a day away from home was difficult, and Yorkshire was slower than other counties in responding to a proclamation by James I in 1618 ordering ale houses to offer food, drink and a bed.

Arthur Young who, in a previous chapter, extolled the virtues of the Yorkshire farmer, was not so enamoured of northern inns. His diary entries of a visit in 1771 were very terse. However, if any of these inns still exists today I am sure the hospitality offered now will be much improved.

> 'The Crown, Rotherham. Very disagreeable and dirty. Hashed venison, potted mackerel, cold ham, cheese and melon. 1 shilling.
>
> The King's Arms, Leeds. Cook dirty. Veal cutlets, tarts and cheese. No beer. 8 pence.
>
> The Nag's Head, Driffield. Civil and cheap. Mutton steaks, ducks, tarts, cheese, mushrooms, capers, walnuts, gherkins, and other pickles. 2 shillings.
>
> The New Inn, Scarborough. Cheap but dirty. Cold ham. Supper: chicken, lobster, anchovie, cheese. 1 shilling and 4 pence (coffee and tea, 6 pence).'

The Hon. John Byng was one of the first tourists to visit Yorkshire for pleasure. He had a passion for waterfalls, but, not content with just admiring, liked to stand under them and get wet. In the summer of 1792 he set out on his great adventure, to visit every waterfall in Yorkshire.

He liked his food, and his diary entries provide us with a clear description of what a wealthy traveller in Yorkshire could expect – and not all of it was good. A traveller of quality might still stay in a large private house owned by someone of the same social class, but you were not guaranteed any degree of comfort. Byng recorded a stay near Barnard Castle: 'I love not the cold of Raby Castle.' Although he did enjoy his visit to Bolton Hall in Wensley, where he ate fresh trout and appreciated the clean bedlinen. Unfortunately, there were not enough grand houses for him during his tour of Yorkshire; so it had to be a public inn most of the time, and these were often just not good enough for a man of his refinement.

Doncaster was a disaster. Byng had a terrible meal at the Angel of stale salmon and boiled beef – standard fare in those days – and 'took against' the landlord, so much so that he recorded in his diary that he would have liked to have given him a good kick! He was pleased with York, 'a good dinner, and a good bottle of port wine at the civil George Inn', but less so with the Crown in Knaresborough, where the fresh trout, just caught at nearby Wetherby, was ruined: 'frying is a difficult and unwholesome cookery.'

Having been upset in Knaresborough, he had better luck at the White Swan at Middleham. 'Below appeared Middleham castle, G. led the horses down the hill into the town to what seemed a sorry inn; however it yielded well, (for they spake of their trout, and their cold larder, with reason), and I was shown into a clean parlour up one pair of stairs. I not only order'd several trout for dinner; but now dictate their cookery, and prevent the frying and the parsley, and the fennel and butter, and substitute boiling and anchovy sauce: as for cold things, they introduce cold ham, cold beef, cold fowl and gooseberry pye … The port wine and the ale seem'd to be equally good. Indeed, I think I have met with very good port wine in this journey.' As much as he enjoyed his stay there it did not stop him from complaining about the bill.

He was in a bad mood on reaching the King's Arms at Askrigg, 'for it was now 5 o'clock and then I got but a baddish dinner, some fried trout, and some tough mutton chops; however the wine was tolerable … Dinner quickly ended – and radishes serv'd up for a desert (sic), as they serve up turnips in Scotland'. Indeed, who would be pleased to see a dish of radishes for pudding rather than a nice fruit pie?

He left Askrigg and made his way westwards, travelling via bleak and desolate Widdale to Ingleton, to view the waterfalls there. By the time he reached the top of Widdale and the Gearstones Inn, which he described as 'the seat of misery, in a desert', he was thoroughly out of sorts. This was made worse by the sight of 'the Scotch fair held upon the heath'. From the late 17th to the late 19th century, thousands of cattle were driven down from Scotland through the dales to be sold in markets in the Midlands. Gearstones was a lively drovers' inn, perhaps a bit too lively for the likes of Byng.

Inside there were further horrors. 'My friend, who knew the house, forced his way through the lower floor, and interned himself in the only wainscoted bedroom upstairs, where at length

The 'curious scenery' from the former Gearstones Inn which so upset the Hon. John Byng. Ingleborough is in the far distance and the Settle to Carlisle railway runs along the flat high ground.

we procured some boil'd slices of stale pork, and some fried eggs, with some wretched beer and brandy, to which my hunger was not equal, and from which my delicacy revolted.'

With his sensibilities thoroughly affronted by the herds of cattle and the squabbling, drunken rabble of rough drovers, the final insult was the 3s 4d bill for the food, ale and brandy: two days' pay in parts of Yorkshire.

Byng was at the mercy of the innkeepers' food, but it was also perfectly acceptable when travelling to buy your own food locally and have the innkeeper cook it for you, or, at times, even do it yourself.

There was good fresh food to be had in Yorkshire. Well-heeled travellers, especially from the south, were amazed at what was on

Central Market, Leeds. (N. Whittock, 1828)

offer at the local markets – fresh lamb, veal and beef, together with salt cod and kippered herring from the east coast, oysters from the mouth of the Humber, and freshwater crawfish, perch, salmon, trout, grayling and eels from the inland rivers – and at prices cheaper than in London. Celia Fiennes, an unusual gentlewoman, who travelled throughout England in the 17th century, wrote in her diary about the large crabs in Beverley market, 'bigger than my two hands, pence apiece, which would have cost sixpence if not a shilling in London'. The fish in the rivers belonged to the landowners, and poaching was a dangerous game, if caught, but a profitable sideline if successful. Much of this poached fish was sold, for obvious reasons, in York market, a good distance away from its source.

Someone shopping in Leeds market in July 1825 had a choice of cherries, raspberries, strawberries, blackcurrants, gooseberries and imported grapes and peaches. However, the difference in the price of home-grown gooseberries at 6d a pound and grapes at 2s 6d a pound meant that few of the working poor ever tasted a grape.

To this day visitors are impressed by the quality of local Yorkshire food. My cousin Marilyn always returns to Virginia Water with a coolbox full of our local meat stowed in her car.

Another friend, flying south from Teesside airport for Christmas, found it not so easy with a Yorkshire goose, dead of course: there was some difficulty with her hand luggage and the airline!

For many who were comfortably off the best food and drink was to be had at home. Laurence Sterne, the witty and eccentric country parson who wrote *Tristram Shandy* and *Sentimental Journey*, enjoyed his food and the pleasures of Shandy Hall. He had 100 chickens in his yard, 'and not a parishioner catches a hare or trout that he brings it as an offering to me'. Life could be sweet as a country parson, and in a letter dated 7th June 1767 he wrote: 'I am as happy as a prince, at Coxwold, and I wish you could see in how princely a manner I live – 'tis a land of plenty. I sit down alone to venison, fish and wild-fowl, or a couple of fowls or ducks with curds, and strawberries and cream, and all the simple plenty which a rich valley under the Hambleton Hills can produce'.

This was a simple life compared to the upper classes, who needed large numbers of servants. Cooks were high in the pecking order of servants, and had staff under them, but needed careful supervision by the mistress of the house. Abstrupus (yes, really) Danby built a manor house at Swinton near Masham in about 1695. He was a Justice of the Peace and a Deputy Lieutenant for the North Riding, a rising man in county affairs. His wife was no less busy, and her copious notes on the duties of the cook maid, housekeeper, chambermaid, butler, dairymaid, house and washing maids meant not a moment of the day was wasted.

'The office of a cook maid as I conceive, is, to take care of the dressing of all the meat fish flesh and foule and make to each their proper sauses belonging to them and to look to the wett larder for the salting of the muscleman beef bacon, and to the preserving of all under her care sweet and good fitt for her Masters table, to wash up and clean all her kitchen vessell and keep them in their places, that none of their number be lost, she is to keep her kitchen, larders, scullery, still house, small beare Seller, the little hall where the servants dine and pantery clean and when we kill a Swine and beefe she is to take care to the washing

Josephine Hopper in the Victorian kitchen at the Dales Countryside Museum, Hawes. On the floor at the front is a large bread crock, above it a marmalade cutter (once the pith was removed this gadget shredded the peel), a raisin seeder and a bean shredder.

the belly to the tups feet and poddings, and when the belly is to be washt the daire maid is to help her do it and to make the poddings, and to help her scouer the pewter.'

Dining for the wealthy had changed since those rowdy days when everyone pitched into the food in the castle hall. By the 17th century the trestle boards had been replaced by a permanent table, and the main meal had moved to 1 pm. The upper classes favoured dining *à la Française*, a style of cuisine with garnishes and elaborately decorated food. The mistress served the soup, which was handed round by the servants, and her husband served the fish. Then two meat dishes were brought on, to be carved by the master at the table. Carving was a gentlemanly skill but the problems become immediately apparent, for carving with skill takes time, and every guest must have an equal amount of good meat. Even today it is a role that men take on with a great deal of fuss: carving knives must be sharpened, hot plates must be at the ready. Some can do it; others just hack away.

The trouble with dining *à la Française* was that everything was on the table and, by the time you were served, the food was cold. Servants passed round the carved meat, the covers were removed from the serving dishes, and the gentlemen helped the ladies to the accompaniments. Servants hovered removing dirty plates and cutlery and replenishing the wine, beer and bread.

The Victorian upper classes came round to favouring dining *à la Russe*, and dinner time moved from late afternoon to early evening. The whole business of carving was now done by a skilled servant operating from the sideboard, with the table given over to elaborate table decorations. French became the language of food in high society; so dinner was a chance to show your social status and sophistication. I suppose the difference in the two styles could be likened to the happy shambles of a family Christmas dinner, with father carving the meat, and too many trimmings and dishes of vegetables to pass round, compared with a formal dinner where it is all done for you by the chef and waiter.

In Ann Holubecki's collection there is a notebook belonging to Letitia Orde Powlett of Bolton Hall, Wensley, in which she recorded, in French, the menus for a week in October 1870. At the top of one page is scrawled 'man cook', but we shall never know who was responsible for the truly gastronomic seven days that

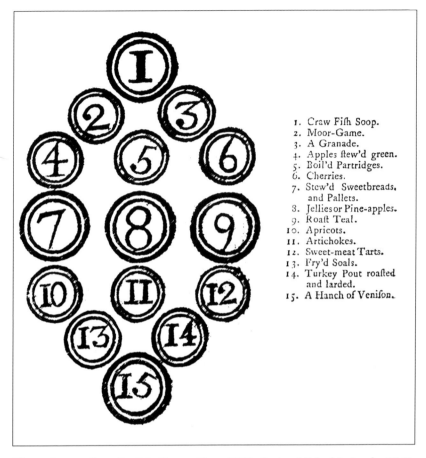

1. Craw Fiſh Soop.
2. Moor-Game.
3. A Granade.
4. Apples ſtew'd green.
5. Boil'd Partridges.
6. Cherries.
7. Stew'd Sweetbreads, and Pallets.
8. Jellies or Pine-apples.
9. Roaſt Teal.
10. Apricots.
11. Artichokes.
12. Sweet-meat Tarts.
13. Fry'd Soals.
14. Turkey Pout roaſted and larded.
15. A Hanch of Veniſon.

The end pages from English Housewifery, 1775, first published in Leeds, 1741. Elizabeth Moxon, who lived in Pontefract, advised on the placing of dishes for a dinner in summer, dining à la Française. (Ann Holubecki Collection)

followed. October is the season for game and much that was eaten that week must have been caught or grown on the estate. There were first courses of fried perch, pike, grilled herrings, sole, cod and salmon; entrées of veal sweetbreads with white sauce, quenelles of rabbit, roast beef, chicken; further courses of beef, lamb, partridge, pheasant, and hare; and lovely desserts of apple loaf with cream, and rich rice puddings. To give you a taste of how the other half dined, the guests at Bolton Hall sat down on October 10th to a dinner of:

First course
game consommé with rice
boiled cod with oyster sauce

Entrées
partridge cutlet with truffles
hare quenelles* with mushrooms

Second course
partridge à la soubise**
roast saddle of mutton

Third course
roast pheasant and grouse

Desserts and Ices
rice pudding with cherries
lemon brioche
ice pudding

(*For those readers needing further explanation, quenelles are chopped meat moulded into balls with egg yolk and breadcrumbs and then fried and often used as a garnish. **Soubise is a sauce made from braised onions with cream.)

All this, and then there was a serious breakfast to face the next morning. Edith Sitwell described breakfast served at 11 am at Londesborough Lodge in Scarborough, the home of her grandmother Lady Londesborough: 'egg and bacon, cold grouse, ham, cold partridge, home-made buns and buttercup-coloured cream and butter, hothouse peaches and grapes'.

A rich chapter indeed, and it is perhaps not surprising that Thomas Beecham (1820–1907) made a fortune with his little pills, famous for curing biliousness, constipation, headaches, and indigestion.

DINING WITHOUT STYLE

A Cheap Dinner

*'Put a sheep's head into warm water, let it soak for 2 or 3
hours, then wash and saw in two from the top. Remove the
brains, cut away a portion of the uncovered part of the skull
and the end of the jaws and put into a stew pan with an onion,
carrots, turnip, celery, some mixed herbs, a few cloves, pepper
and salt and 3 quarts of water. Let the whole simmer gently for
about 2 hours. For serving, lay the head on a dish with the
vegetables, skim off the fat and pour the broth round the head.'*

Recipe from Brunswick Street, York

'But what about the workers?' I hear you cry. If the last
chapter was too rich for your liking, there were many in
Yorkshire who could only dream of a dinner with five
courses. The West Riding weavers suffered particularly hard times
during the transition from working at home on their handlooms to
working in the factories on power looms.

The Yorkshire writer J. Keighley Snowden, son of the
headmaster of Bingley Grammar School, wrote in 1896 *The Web of
an Old Weaver*. The writing has echoes of those comic sketches
where two men try and outdo each other as to the poverty of their
childhood: 'Ee, I walked 10 miles to school wi' no shoes and only
went when my brother didn't want the trousers … ' 'By heck, that's
nothing I walked 20 miles …'

Snowden, who read mathematics at Cambridge, cannot have
suffered the hardship he portrayed, but must have seen plenty in
and around Bingley: 'When I was a little lad I found a penny once.
There were seven of us lads in the family, and we took daily turns
at scraping the porridge pan. I went to my father and told him
about this penny, and said I would give it him if I might scrape the

pan three times running. And that way I would have wared (spent) it. We had nought but 'porridge and stop' then, and sometimes we had not that. I can tell of my mother fainting one morning when she had served us all round and left herself none; and that morning I had scraped the pan.'

On the other hand, it paid a farmer to feed his workers, for how else would they manage to work their long hours? Single men and women were hired at the Martinmas hiring fairs (November 23rd) for a year, and generally lived in. The unmarried girl would help the farmer's wife in the kitchen with cooking and housework, and then work outside when she had a spare minute. An hour's work before a substantial breakfast at 6 am of cold meat and fruit pies was followed by a generous midday dinner of beef or bacon, Yorkshire pudding, suet or savoury pudding, washed down with large amounts of tea. Supper was more cold meat, fruit pies and bread and butter to send you to bed on a full stomach. Once a farm worker married there might be a cottage nearby available for him and his new wife, but if he continued to eat at the farmhouse at midday, rather than return home, the farmer docked his wages for the food eaten.

Many people left the country to seek work in the industrial towns. The houses built for the newly arrived poor to rent were cramped, back to back terraces. Some could afford to live in one room only, in a courtyard teeming with families, who had no option but to live in unsanitary, overcrowded conditions, often with their animals. A clergyman and a doctor, visiting the poorer parts of York for 'A Report on the State of York' in 1844, recorded in detail the general filthiness they found:

> 'Backcourt 46, in a filthy state; the privies running over and allowed to accumulate, and altogether it is very confined; there is also a pig sty, hen roost, and cow house, closely attached to the house.'

York had once been the 'capital of the North', the rich and landed gentry taking houses in the city as a change from their country estates. Here they enjoyed the pleasures of the races, grand balls in the Assembly Rooms, the theatre, concerts and card games. As is the way of fashion, by the mid 1800s, York was a decaying city, the aristocracy moving on in search of fresh entertainments.

The lower classes took their pleasures where they could, and for a short time in the early 1800s gormandizing or food eating contests, on which you could place a wager, excited certain sections of York society. This must have appealed to young men, as it still would today: a hot room crowded with sweaty bodies, alcohol, bets on the outcome, cheering and coarse comments.

Eating vast amounts of indigestible food against the clock was bound to have consequences, and the *York Chronicle* reported the death in 1817 of 'Mutton-eating Bandy Billy of the parish of Newbiggin, a man long distinguished for the voracity of his appetite'. He was found dead shortly after failing to digest a 10lb leg of mutton, 2 large bunches of turnips, much bread, and a gallon of porter.

In 1825 William Cook, a York labourer commonly known as 'Bacon Billy', held the citizens of York in thrall in a succession of contests. The *York Courant* reported, under the headline 'More Gormandizing': 'The man whose stomachic abilities were detailed by us a few weeks ago, was showing off at a great gorge, at Mr Vause's, the Wind Mill, without Castlegate Postern last night. This person, who, from his feats in this way, seems to partake of the nature of a Boa Constrictor, had engaged to devour a goose in the space of one hour. Accordingly a fine one, weighing 8½ lb. was spitted and served up with a due proportion of sage, onions &c. This morsel was dispatched in 34 minutes, when the gentleman called for a remove, and a giblet pie, including the blood was set before him. This also disappeared in decent time, and the bottomless paunch yearned for 2 lbs of cheeses, which, however, were not provided. Numbers of persons from this city, and even from the neighbouring villages, were present at this delicate exhibition.'

We hear of him once more when he managed a roasted sucking pig, but in the manner of these things fickle fashion moved on and we too must leave this branch of show business and return to more normal eating.

The food you ate was plain and cheap; the ingredients even plainer:

Queer Times Pudding
from Wakefield, 1916

1 cupful each of breadcrumbs, flour, currants, sugar
2 ozs suet
pinch of salt
2 teaspoons baking powder

Mix all together with a little milk and steam for two hours.

If the woman of the house was a good cook, she generally made a meal with what was available, the main purpose being to fill you up, rather than tickle your taste buds. No bit of an animal was left uneaten, from the head to the foot or cow's heel. Brawn was a real treat, but the pig's ears and tongue took some cooking. Tripe, the stomach lining of a cow in all its ineffable forms, was bought ready cooked from the local tripe shop. Honeycomb tripe, so called because of its appearance, was more digestible, especially for those who were ill, and was served up to the invalid with onions and white sauce. However, I am describing here 'gourmet' cooking, for in most cases the staple diet of the working class consisted of potatoes, porridge, pig, Yorkshire pudding, bread and butter, sweetened tea, oatmeal, soups, hashes, anything you grew yourself or could pick for free and ... more porridge. This was in a good week.

Dr Johnson in his *Dictionary of the English Language* (1755) was very dismissive of the staple food here in the North, and he liked to annoy the Scots: 'Oats: A grain, which in England is generally given to horses, but in Scotland supports the people.' To this could be added 'and Yorkshire, Lancashire, Westmorland and Staffordshire'. The reason is simple, as oats will grow on high ground, in a wet climate, and on poor soil.

Oats were ground between gritstones for oatmeal, which was used in oatcakes and added as bulk to a distressing number of dishes. The coarse oats for porridge needed soaking overnight before cooking and the resulting chewiness would not perhaps be to our taste today as we are used to refined rolled oats. To save on fuel the very poor cooked a double amount at breakfast time, saving some for midday in a stone jar, which was stored under the bedcovers to keep warm until needed. We now know of the excellent health properties of oats: lowering blood pressure, reducing cholesterol and even improving one's sex drive, but even if people had known this, it would have been little consolation for the dispiriting monotony of the oat.

For many in Yorkshire, homemade oatcakes, spread with butter, were part of childhood and remembered with pleasure. I have only eaten a modern, bought oatcake, and it was hard to decide which would be tastier: a slice of the packaging it came in or the oatcake. Perhaps it was different in the past. The basic recipe does not inspire confidence, and I cannot bring myself to put it in the chapter on Yorkshire delicacies.

Oatcake (Havercake)

1½ cups of oatmeal
1 cup of flour
a knob of lard
salt

Mix ingredients together and add cold water to make a stiff paste. Roll out and bake on a griddle over a moderate heat until the edges begin to curl. Turn over and cook the other side. If they are to keep they should be propped up to dry by the fire on a small easel known as a cake stool.

The havercakes or haverbread, (*hafri* means oats in Old Norse), eaten in the northern dales were thin and crisp and cooked on backstones. A *bakst'n* was originally a flat stone which was heated in the fire. This concept evolved into a cast-iron plate built over a firebox, or, for home baking, a portable round iron griddle that hung over the fire. The oatcakes were hung to dry over a wooden rack, a *breead-fleg*, suspended from the ceiling, and could be kept for some time. It was said that those existing mainly on oatcakes always had good teeth; the roughness must have kept them clean.

In West Riding towns a different type of oatcake known as a 'riddlecake' was still baked on a backstone. Riddlecakes, a bakery product, were long, oval and soft, and made from a batter which included yeast. They sound nicer, especially if eaten straightaway

Woman making oatcakes. The backstone or bakestone is on the left of the fireplace. The cooked oatcakes were cooled on the cloth over the chair on the floor and then hung on the bread creel suspended from the ceiling. (From George Walker's The Costume of Yorkshire, *first published in 1814)*

The recruiting sergeants of the 33rd Regiment, formed during the American War of Independence in the Halifax area, led the way, waving a sword with a havercake on the end. They were known as the Havercake Lads. (From George Walker's The Costume of Yorkshire, *1814)*

rolled up with butter and treacle. At one time there were said to be 40 bakeries in Bradford, and the bakers travelled the streets with baskets of oatcakes over each arm.

Whatever the form of the oatcake, there was an awful lot of it eaten, and for a short time in 1800 it even became a symbol of working class revolt. At a time of high food prices Benjamin Wilson, waving an oatcake on a stick, incited a mob to riot. This sort of behaviour was not tolerated, and he spent some time in Wakefield Gaol.

Which brings me nicely to the food poor Benjamin Wilson would have enjoyed while spending time at His Majesty George IV's 'pleasure'. It was probably better than he was eating on the outside, but the rules for the government of the house of correction at Wakefield in 1801 still relied heavily on oatmeal. There is an awful lot of porridge in this chapter!

	BREAKFAST	DINNER	SUPPER
SUNDAY	One Quart Oatmeal Pottage. Half a Pound of Bread.	Half a Pound Beef, One Pound Vegetables or Potatoes.	*Same as* Breakfast
MONDAY	– *Same* –	One Quart of Broth from Beef of Yesterday with herbs. Half a Pound of Bread.	– *Same* –
TUESDAY	– *Same* –	Quarter of a Pound of Cheese. Half a Pound of Bread.	– *Same* –
WEDNESDAY	– *Same* –	One Quart of Rice and Oatmeal Pottage. Half a Pound of Bread.	– *Same* –
THURSDAY	– *Same* –	*Same as* Sunday.	– *Same* –
FRIDAY	– *Same* –	*Same as* Monday.	– *Same* –
SATURDAY	– *Same* –	One Quart Stew of Heads and Bones.	– *Same* –

NOTE: Breakfast delivered at eight o'clock in summer, and at nine o'clock in winter; Dinner at twelve o'clock; Supper delivered at eight o'clock in summer, and at six o'clock in winter.

No pigs, fowls, or other animals must be kept within the walls of the prison, except the keeper's dog, for his security.

How they must have looked forward to Sunday, and the expressions for being in prison 'doing porridge' or 'doing stir' has everything to do with the monotony of the food.

Without oatmeal the poor were lost, and bad weather meant failing crops. When combined with rising food prices, this meant that life spiralled downwards. In remote Wensleydale the doughty Dalesmen tackled these problems with practical help, not looking for outside assistance. The *Wensleydale Advertiser* of 5th January 1847 reported that an Oatmeal Fund had been set up for the poor of the area. 'The high price of provisions and the severe weather ... rendered it imperatively necessary that some effort should be made to ameliorate the very distressed condition of the working classes of the neighbourhood. The call has been nobly responded to; and we are glad to state that between £50 and £60 have already been subscribed.'

The following week the *Wensleydale Advertiser* reported: 'Potatoes, which constitute so large a part of the food of the people throughout the kingdom, are more than double their ordinary price ... and bacon, ham and pork, which are likewise very largely consumed in ordinary times, are now at extravagant prices, owing to the supply of pigs from Ireland having almost ceased.' (This was the knock-on effect of events across the Irish Sea between 1845 and 1850, when the disastrous potato famines caused starvation and death in Ireland, and mass emigration to America.)

In all, 120 heads of families, which with family members meant nearly 400 people, registered with the Oatmeal Fund and were instructed to be at the National Schoolroom in Hawes to 'receive their respective portions of oatmeal (or flour for the aged)'. There is something admirable about the self-help and organization in those hard times, for without it the only alternative was the dreaded workhouse.

For most of us any knowledge we have of the workhouse comes from Charles Dickens' *Oliver Twist* and Lionel Bart's musical *Oliver*.

Only the stonyhearted remain untouched by the orphaned Oliver asking for more gruel. For those unfamiliar with just what exactly constitutes gruel, also known as broth or, in Yorkshire, Bastille soup, the recipe is as follows:

Workhouse Gruel

For each gallon of meat liquor in which the meat was boiled, add 4 ozs of oatmeal, parsley, pepper and salt.

Yet, although the fear and shame of the workhouse hung over many families, with loss of liberty and separation, in hard times the workhouse charity meant you ate more than those still working on the outside. The New Poor Law Act of 1834 positively discouraged anyone from seeking respite in the workhouse, but the wage paid to those working on the land and in factories was so low that very often families were close to starving in spite of a weekly wage. A Board of Guardians was elected with responsibility for running the whole show, and they were always mindful of the money paid, by way of the poor rate, by the wealthier citizens of the parish.

Some workhouses were humanely run and others were a cruel disgrace. The Poor Law Board of the Barnsley Union in 1853 set out quite a decent weekly diet. Men had more bread than women at each meal, with porridge invariably for breakfast and supper. Three days a week for the midday dinner there was a fairly generous 16 ounces of hash or stew; on three days there were four ounces of meat with potatoes or vegetables; and on Saturday you looked forward to two ounces of cheese and suet pudding.

'We, the Poor Law Board, do hereby Order and Direct that the Paupers maintained in the Workhouse of the Barnsley Union ... a sufficient quantity of tea for breakfast and for supper, not exceeding one pint per meal, sweetened with an allowance of sugar, not exceeding half an ounce to each pint of tea ... Children under the age of twelve years, resident in the said Workhouse, shall be dieted with such food and in such manner as the said Guardians shall direct; and that children between twelve and sixteen years of age shall be allowed the same quantities as are prescribed for women.'

The workhouses were often run by retired military men used to giving orders and having them obeyed. On the wall of the Methodist chapel in Bainbridge is a fine memorial tablet to James Mason, who died aged 56 in 1840. 'He served 12 years in the Army and for the last 7 years of that period was Sergeant in the First Scotch Royals and was twice Orderly to his Royal Highness the Duke of Kent. For 22 years he faithfully discharged the Important duties of Governor of the Incorporated Workhouse at Bainbridge.' When I remarked on this to a retired gentleman who had lived all his life in the area, he recalled the only thing his mother had told him about the workhouse was that the inmates were not allowed butter, only margarine.

The workhouse in Leeds seems to have been well run, although the food was not so plentiful as at Barnsley. Sheffield Workhouse was a shambles, with the breakfast porridge and supper eaten while sitting on your bed and the adults eating first, with the leftovers given to the children. Knaresborough Workhouse does not sound too bad; the inmates were taken to Harrogate races and treated to gingerbread. At Pickering you were allowed a tot of rum if you were poorly, while the Leyburn Workhouse was efficiently run by 'a gallant veteran' who allowed 'every possible indulgence'.

There is a story about a kindly master of the Keighley Workhouse who toured the dining room at mealtimes to enquire on the well being of the inmates. One old lady complained bitterly to him about the food, 'Look at this,' she wailed, holding up a small, shrivelled, blackened round bean. 'These kidney beans are the worst I've ever had. How am I expected to eat this? ' The master took the bean from her and put it between his teeth and tried to bite it: the bean was rock solid. 'You are quite right,' he said. 'This is quite disgraceful, and you cannot possibly be expected to eat this.' The old woman looked triumphant, 'That's what I've been telling you – and it's been through me twice already!'

One institution of which we all have experience is school. Everyone can tell a story or give an opinion on school dinners. For some they were loathsome messes, for others the only square meal of the day, offering also the hope of 'seconds'. School dinners now are a *cause célèbre*, with TV chef Jamie Oliver highlighting how little goodness there is in the pizzas, re-formed turkey meat and chips which are catapulting a generation into obesity.

Being overweight was seldom a problem in the past, and school dinners were only provided if you were at boarding school. Otherwise you went home or took your own food to school for the midday meal, and if you were lucky the teacher boiled some water for a cup of cocoa or tea. Often you went outside to eat and if it was raining you spent the afternoon slowly steaming in wet clothes.

The Brontë sisters had plain food at home in the parsonage at Haworth. Their mother died when they were young and a servant cooked for them: porridge, milk, bread and butter for breakfast, dinner at 2 pm of roast or boiled meat with some kind of milk pudding to follow, and tea in the early evening. The sisters were sent off to a boarding school for the daughters of clergymen at Cowan Bridge near Kirkby Lonsdale where, as at most of these establishments, the food was meagre and badly cooked.

More than 20 years later Charlotte Brontë gave a vivid account in her novel *Jane Eyre* of the loathsome school food, drawing on her miserable time at Cowan Bridge. Jane is sent to Lowood Institution, a charity school for orphans, a grim place with such poor food rations that the older girls bullied the younger ones out of their brown bread and coffee at teatime. Supper on Jane Eyre's first day at school was water and a portion of thin oaten cake. At breakfast the next morning, 'I perceived I had got in hand a nauseous mess: burnt porridge is almost as bad as rotten potatoes: famine itself soon sickens over it. The spoons were moved slowly; I saw each girl taste her food and try to swallow it; but in most cases the effort was soon relinquished. Breakfast was over, and none had breakfasted.'

Dinner was no better. 'The odour which now filled the refectory was scarcely more appetizing than that which had regaled our nostrils at breakfast: the dinner was served in two huge tin-plated vessels, whence rose a strong steam redolent of rancid fat. I found the mess to consist of indifferent potatoes and strange shreds of rusty meat, mixed and cooked together.'

Whatever your thoughts on school dinners, Yorkshire people must be proud that the first school meals in Britain were provided by a group of energetic, philanthropic businessmen in Bradford. In 1890 the Cinderella Club was started by volunteers responding to the alarming poverty in the city's slums. Weekly free teas and entertainments for 5,000 children were soon followed by *clogging*, a supply of secondhand clothes, and outings to the country provided by Mrs Titus Salt of Salt's Mills. The economic depression in the early 1900s, following the Boer War, led to even more children being fed breakfast and a midday meal, paid for by a special mayor's fund. A report by the Cinderella Club to Bradford Education Committee in 1904 estimated there were between 2,000 and 3,000 children who were always hungry.

With the passing of the Education (Provision of Meals) Act in 1906, Bradford tackled the problem of feeding its school children, which in fact it had been unlawful to do up until then. With an extra halfpenny on the rates, the Education Committee set about costing a variety of school dinners. The cheapest dinner in 1908 was green pea and vegetable soup, bread, and boiled jam roly-poly pudding at 9d each. A medium priced dinner was Yorkshire cheese pudding, bread, peas, bean gravy, and buttered rice, costing 11d, and the most expensive dinner, a nourishing meat and potato pie, bread, milk pudding and stewed fruit, cost 1s 4d.

We should be grateful to those early pioneers of school dinners, but few of my generation seem to have happy memories. Many have spoken of the humiliation and divisive nature of free meals for the poor, with some schools making no effort to be discreet about those who did not pay. We paid on a Monday for the meals and milk for the week, and being a milk monitor was seen as the first step on a career in management. In winter the milk was often frozen, with ice spilling out of the glass bottles. The cardboard tops had a hole in the middle for the straw, and these were saved for making pompoms with bits of spare wool. I have quite forgotten why we wanted all those pompoms.

Grace said before eating was generally 'For what we are about to receive, may the Lord make us truly thankful/grateful'. Most of us were decidedly ungrateful. From a phone-in programme I once did on BBC Radio York, there was a consensus amongst the callers that the weekly menu for Yorkshire schools in the 1950s and early 60s went something like this:

Monday: stew with huge lumps of gristle which you transferred into your handkerchief, or if you were a girl tucked into the pocket of your regulation school knickers. Vegetables were mashed potatoes and well cooked watery cabbage.

Tuesday: mince, cooked in such a way as to make it slimy and an odd grey colour, and more cabbage.

Wednesday: roast dinner. Hurrah!

Thursday: mince again, but with pastry on top. School pastry was referred to as 'tiles', a reference, I suppose, to the fact you could roof a house with it.

Friday: fish – echoes of a more religious past, and the cod boiled in milk was a true penance.

With the school dinner ladies' 'signature dish' of well cooked cabbage, no wonder this was the smell of schooldays.

The food was often worse in fee-paying schools, and one lady recalled that steamed suet pudding was always known as 'Matron's leg'. There is a story about a private girls' school in Yorkshire run by two elderly ladies. During the Second World War it was difficult feeding the girls, so the school's odd job man spent all his time shooting rabbits in the woods. Rabbit, in a variety of forms, was the only meat they ever ate.

The puddings were the best part of school dinners, especially gypsy tart, a sweet mixture of brown sugar and condensed milk baked in a pastry case; jam tart and custard, known as 'hammer and chisel tart'; spotted Dick or dog; and rhubarb and custard. Not so good were sago pudding, known to everyone as 'frogspawn', or tapioca pudding and rice pudding with solid lumps. Any pudding with golden syrup was a disappointment, as the syrup was watered down in the interests of economy. Puddings at my husband's school in Leeds were referred to as 'scabby matter custard and green phlegm pie'.

A former pupil at the old Yorebridge Grammar School in Askrigg described – and these are her words – 'a diabolical chocolate pudding covered in a revolting pink sauce'. Dinners were eaten in the domestic science room, and each table had a rolling out board underneath. She would carefully place the noxious mess on the rolling board, smooth it out, and gently push the board back under the table.

If I have unintentionally blackened the reputation of any retired

school cooks, I apologize. Of course nothing was ever as awful as
the old schoolboy rhyme from South Yorkshire suggests:

Dead dogs' giblets, green cats' eyes,
All mixed together in a snot and bogie pie.
Horses' skin all green and thick,
All washed down with a cup of cold sick.

IF IT'S FEBRUARY, IT MUST BE COLLOPS

Give us Lord, a bit o' Sun,
A bit o' work and a bit of fun.
Give us in all the fuss and sputter
Our daily bread and a bit o' butter.

Prayer on the wall of the Crown Inn at Askrigg

In the distant past we were never far away from famine. If part of the yearly cycle of growing and harvesting collapsed, so too did our ability to survive. The summer was the season of plenty, but, once the harvest was gathered and the fresh food finished, you ate your animals. Geese and hens grazed on harvest gleanings and, like the fattened pigs, were killed one by one and eaten. You hoped the dried and salted meat would see you through a harsh winter, but if spring came late there was no alternative but to kill the animals kept for breeding, and the farming cycle failed. With no new animals to breed from or to work the fields, famine quickly followed.

Until recently people still had the urge to preserve for the coming winter. A good Yorkshire woman prepared for the worst and wasted nothing; the year for her was defined by the food in season, and traditions and festivals throughout Yorkshire were linked with foods that were either seasonal or to be eaten on special occasions.

January, and the fields are bare, and the Blessing of the Plough still occurs in the great abbey church at Selby. The abbey plough, once owned by a champion ploughman of England from Camblesforth, is still there in the abbey, and the ceremony on Plough Sunday, the first Sunday after Epiphany, is a reminder of our old links with, and dependence on, the land. On the first Monday after Twelfth Night the farmhands returned from their homes to the farms for the new working year, and the young men dragged the plough to the local church, singing, dancing and begging for money. If that was not forthcoming, then those lining the route threw small cheesecakes to the young men, who caught them in their aprons to be eaten later with mulled ale and beer.

In more religious times when the Church wielded enormous power and influence, the period of Lent from Ash Wednesday to Easter Eve was the season for fasting, penitence and doing without meat. In this period of 40 days' abstinence there were a number of times when a little break would be taken for a treat and before it even started it was good to have a party.

In parts of the Catholic world the days before Ash Wednesday are a time of celebration, colour and carnivals, but here in Yorkshire they did things differently. On Collop Monday Yorkshire children called round to demand, rather ungraciously, I think, 'Pray dame, a collop, or we'll give you a whallop.' You were given a slice of home cured bacon or ham to take home and enjoy with a fried egg. The fat was kept for the next day, Shrove Tuesday (once called 'Fastens'), for cooking the pancakes. By the 1920s the slice of bacon was replaced in industrial Huddersfield with a handful of pennies thrown to waiting part-time workers at 12.15 pm, when the colloping was supposed to stop.

In York Minster the apprentices and journeymen climbed the tower and rang the bells at 11 o' clock on Shrove Tuesday to announce that work had finished. In Richmond, Pickering and Scarborough the church bells tolled the 'pancake bell', which had replaced the old 'shriving bell', the call to confess your sins. Children finished school and returned home for their pancakes, eaten with sugar, treacle, and lemon (or vinegar, if you were poor). An old superstition held that eating pancakes on Shrove Tuesday ensured you had money all year.

There was an element of anarchy on this day, as a Yorkshire custom had children locking the school doors and keeping the teacher outside until he or she had granted them a holiday. On the 10th of February 1880 the headmaster of Carperby School noted in the school logbook: 'Shrove Tuesday was observed by the children as barring-out day, which the big boys attended with great glee to obtain a half holiday.' Reading other comments in his school logbook, here was a man not altogether happy in his work. The master at Sedbergh Grammar School had every reason to enjoy Shrove Tuesday, as that was the day he collected 4½d from each boy to be used to buy a fighting cock!

Ash Wednesday and the start of Lent: early Christians sprinkled ashes over their heads or marked their forehead with ash, as an act of repentance. In parts of Yorkshire the word *ash* was mistakenly understood as *hash*, and rather than an act of repentance you ate hashed potatoes instead. A mistake anyone could make. If you were not quite ready to start the fasting, there was another celebratory dish for Ash Wednesday, which used up the last of the eggs and fruit. Any kind of batter is popular in Yorkshire and *fruttaces*, or fritters, are more luxurious than the Shrove Tuesday pancakes.

Fruttaces

2 eggs
8 ozs plain flour
1 oz yeast
2½ ozs each of currants and caster sugar
2 medium grated apples
½ oz candied peel
a little nutmeg
a cup of tepid milk

Mix all the dry ingredients. Dissolve the yeast in the milk and pour into the middle of the dry mix and add the eggs. Cover and leave to rise overnight. Drop a spoonful at a time into boiling lard in a frying pan. Drain and sprinkle with sugar.

Lent was interrupted on the fourth Sunday for Mothering Sunday, also known as Refreshment Sunday and Simnel Sunday. Families spent the day together and attended their 'mother' church. Farm workers, apprentices and maid servants left their masters and returned home for the day, bringing with them a rich simnel cake. The cake was cooked with a layer of marzipan inside. Once the cake had cooled another layer was added, on the top, and decorated with eleven round marzipan balls to represent the Apostles, except Judas.

The fifth Sunday in Lent, Passion Sunday, was once known by other names associated with sorrow and mourning, such as Care Sunday. In Yorkshire it was also called *Carlin'* Sunday, since, as a further act of penance, it was the custom to eat dried peas, or *carlings*, which had been soaked in cold water overnight and then fried in butter and eaten with salt and pepper. Pubs put a dish of salted *carlings* on the counter for customers to help themselves – not much of a generous gesture, as the salt made the drinker even thirstier (peanuts and crisps do the same). Young people believed that the person to eat the last pea in the dish would be the first to be married.

In the north-east of the county they preferred their peas hot and sweet, with brown sugar and a drop of rum. Rum was a favourite in these parts, and there were ample supplies, as widespread rum-smuggling was reputed to go on around Skinningrove, Staithes and Robin Hood's Bay. Too many peas and your digestive system paid the price: 'Carlin' Sunday, Fartin' Monday'.

There are various theories how the peas got their name. The ancient Greeks believed that peas and beans contained the souls of the dead. Here in Yorkshire it is said the peas take their name from a Captain Carlin whose ship sunk off the Holderness coast near Hull, a remote stretch of coast constantly eroded by the sea, and the cargo of peas was plundered by hungry locals. A similar story is told of another shipwreck, further north, where the starving villagers of Carlin How, just inland between Staithes and Saltburn, looted another cargo of peas.

Palm Sunday, the sixth Sunday in Lent, was also known until the 1930s as Fig Sunday or Fig Pudding Day. The name probably referred to the Gospel story of Jesus cursing a barren fig tree on the way to Jerusalem. In Yorkshire it was the custom to eat solid and filling fig puddings or pies, but the four-hour cooking time means few of us now would take the trouble.

Fig Sunday Pudding

12 ozs finely grated breadcrumbs
6 ozs each of suet and sugar
a teacup of milk
1 egg
8 ozs figs
nutmeg

Chop the suet and figs very fine. Mix the breadcrumbs and suet, and then add the figs, sugar, nutmeg, well-beaten egg and milk. Boil in a pudding basin for four hours. Eat with a sweet sauce.

Easter can fall anytime between 25th March and 25th April, depending on the first full moon on or after the spring equinox.

Hot cross buns hanging in an Askrigg kitchen, one for each of the last 20 years – good luck or once believed to be a useful medicine for skin infections or digestive disorders.

For a Christian festival there are a remarkable number of superstitions surrounding Easter. The hot cross buns baked on Good Friday were believed to have healing powers and, if one was kept back, it would bring good luck to the house for the next year and never grow mouldy. Farmers hung one up in the barn to protect the farm from rats. Originally the buns were eaten hot and fresh for breakfast, which meant someone had to be up early to bake them.

Fridays meant fish, and never more so than on Good Friday, but the other traditional Good Friday dish made from herbs is no longer eaten, and perhaps we can understand why, although if you were hungry it would fill a hole.

Whitby Herb Pudding

1 pint each of breadcrumbs and milk
2 eggs
4 ozs finely chopped suet
2 teaspoons chopped parsley
salt and pepper

Whisk the eggs and place with the milk and salt and pepper in a pan and bring slowly to the boil, stirring all the time. As the mixture thickens, add the suet, breadcrumbs and parsley. Put in a greased pie dish and bake in a hot oven until brown.

Pace eggs were part of every child's Easter in the north. The word *pace* is from Old French *pasque* 'Easter', ultimately from Hebrew *pesach* 'Passover'. For early Christians the egg was a symbol of resurrection and new life. The eggs were dyed in boiling water with gorse blossom for yellow, cochineal for red, or, as I remember, wrapped with onion skins held in place with newspaper and string. The marbled effects are lovely.

You rolled the pace eggs down a hill on Easter Sunday or Monday, and, if they reached the bottom without a crack, it was a sign of good fortune for the next year. Others played a game rolling an egg to try and crack or *jowp* your opponent's or holding the egg tightly in your hand while someone brought their egg smartly down onto yours, again trying to crack it – a bit like conkers, but without the string.

Easter Sunday is still a time for a special family meal of spring lamb or pork and, because of the glut of eggs left from the Lent fasting, baked custards and cheesecakes. 'On Heeaster Sunda' we've Peeast Eggs an' lots o' Kustods teea.' The prevailing cold wind on the east coast at this time of the year was called a 'custard wind'.

The Whitsuntide Sunday school treat was just that: a treat. For most children it was the only time you travelled beyond your village. If you lived within a couple of hours of Whitby, Scarborough, Filey or Redcar you had the excitement of a charabanc or motor coach ride for a picnic, games and hymn singing on the beach. Inland, a favourite Sunday school spot was Brimham Rocks, near Ripon, with its strange shaped rocks for climbing on and far views of the Dales to the west and the moors rising to the east. Mothers went on the trips and the Anglican or Nonconformist clergyman from your church or chapel. There were bats and balls, games of hide and seek among the rocks and a picnic tea; it was a day to remember.

Before the motor coach, children could only march. The *Wensleydale Advertiser* in May 1847 reported on the Wesleyan Sunday School treat in Middleham:

'The scholars of this school were, as usual, on Whitmonday, regaled with tea and spice cake. In the early part of the afternoon they walked round the town, attended by the teachers and sung appropriate hymns in the principal street; after tea, a suitable address was given and the party broke up very much pleased with the entertainment.'

A 1970s Women's Institute cookbook claimed that plum bread was made for the York Sunday School scholars at least 60 years ago.

Sunday School Treat Plum Bread

2 lbs flour
½ lb lard
1 lb sugar
¼ lb golden syrup
¼ lb candied peel
1½ lbs currants
2 moderately heaped teaspoons
of bicarbonate of soda and some milk

Rub the fat into the flour. Add the other ingredients and mix to a soft dough with milk. Bake in a slow oven.

Children always enjoyed a bread and treacle race. I know of one in Askrigg that took place until recently. Boys and girls had separate races. They stood in a row on top of a high wall and each was handed a thick slice of homemade bread covered in treacle. The first one to eat it, jump off the wall, and then whistle (to prove they had an empty mouth) was the winner. Older villagers remember during the Second World War having the race in a field and, because there was no treacle available, eating the bread with molasses instead – 60 years on they still recall the disgusting taste of the molasses and the difficulty in swallowing it.

A health and safety risk assessment would condemn this race now for (a) standing on a wall, (b) possible choking on the bread, (c) jumping off the wall – and (d) there is probably a danger attached to whistling, too.

The feast of St Wilfred, the 7th-century patron saint of Ripon Cathedral, is celebrated during Wilfra Week, in August. As an example of Yorkshire generosity it was once the custom for women to rise at 4 am to bake jam and lemon curd tarts, and passers by were invited to help themselves to the tarts, placed on a large dish just inside the door of the smaller houses.

The Wilfra tart we know now is a more sophisticated affair with sweetened sliced apple sprinkled with Wensleydale cheese baked in a pastry case.

For farmers a good harvest in July and August depended on the weather. A dry wind was needed if crops of wheat, barley and oats were to be successfully gathered in. It was a time of intensive work when every able bodied man, woman and child worked in the fields. The farmer's wife was just as busy back in the farmhouse kitchen feeding the workers, and the children ran to and from the fields carrying food and drink. Huge machines cut a field now and have it stored away in a couple of hours, but in the past harvest time needed as many able bodied people as you could feed. Although the work was hard and hot, the food supplied by the farmer's wife on the short picnic breaks in the fields was eaten with relish. Homemade bread and local cheese, freshly made oatcakes, rich pastry *nodden* cakes, and large slices of thirst-quenching gooseberry pie with lashings of sweet tea or a drop of beer.

Once a custom in the Craven district of Yorkshire for newcomers on Midsummer Eve 'to set out a plentiful repast before their doors, of cold beef, bread, cheese, and ale'. Those neighbours who wished to be friendly would 'sit down and partake of their hospitable fare, and thus eat and drink themselves into intimacy'. (From George Walker's The Costume of Yorkshire, *1814)*

The traditional harvest loaf made for the Harvest Festival Service at Stalling Busk church.

The Stanger family of Redmire in Wensleydale resting from harvesting in the late 1940s – a moment of quiet enjoyment in a busy day, with good food eaten properly with bowls and spoons. Alas, I cannot say who took this delightful picture. (Ann Holubecki Collection)

When the crops were cut, the farmer provided the *kern*, or 'churn', supper of cakes, ale and cream from the churn, though the workers preferred ale to cream. The *mell* supper was given after all the crops were safely gathered in. (The word *mel* or *mjol* occurs in both Danish and Icelandic and is simply translated as a 'meal'.) The old Yorkshire mell suppers were jolly affairs, usually held in a barn, with eating, drinking, dancing and singing to fiddles.

> *'An what Mell suppers there was then!*
> *All t' warkfooaks went seea smart;*
> *They'd tea, an beef, an ham, an then*
> *They'd lots o' keeak an' tart.'*

As so often in Victorian times there was disapproval of the heavy drinking and high spirits of the mell suppers, and local clergy preferred their farming community to give thanks in a more sober style in church at a Harvest Festival service. However, Yorkshire people have not lost their ability to have a good time, and many communities still enjoy fine food and fellowship at a harvest supper.

The hedgerows in August and September are said to indicate the winter to come: 'Many hips and haws, many frosts and snows.' Once upon a time everything that grew was made into a pie or jam: hedgerow blackberries, damsons, elderberries, moorland bilberries; garden gooseberries, plums and apples. Tom Roe of Whitby remembered as a boy during the Second World War gathering wild strawberries by the basketful to make jam; given the size of a wild strawberry, he would have needed some patience. Strawberries grew in the fields round Staithes, flowering on the cinder and scrub land where once there had been ironstone mines. Blackberries too were there for the picking, for jam or, even better, bramble suet pudding.

Tom Roe's Bramble Suet Pudding

Line a bowl with suet pastry. Fill with freshly picked blackberries. Fold the pastry over the top. Steam for a couple of hours.

If you did not have a bowl handy you simply lined a tea towel with the suet pastry instead and it would do just as well.

In Victorian times children went back to school in the middle of August. This did not stop them from continuing to enjoy themselves, and attendance at school was often inconvenient, as recorded in the Carperby school log by their long suffering teacher.

'1894 August 24th Leyburn Agricultural Show accounts for many absent today.
August 30th Holiday for Sunday School picnic.
September 14th 3.30pm took the children to Haw bank to gather nuts.
September 28th Poor attendance due to Redmire feast.
October 5th 3 days this week have been devoted to Aysgarth feast so that attendances were much decreased. It is well that the tales of feasts is almost told.
October 12th Small attendance today on account of Leyburn fair.

The Redmire cheesecake gatherers at Redmire feast at the turn of the last century. Were any of the missing Carperby school children in this picture? Originally young village men marched round the village with blackened faces begging for curd tarts. (Ann Holubecki Collection)

October 19th Fire lighted for first time. Some children absent at Hawes fair.'

We can understand why, according to the school log, there was a high turnover of teachers.

The end of summer and autumn or 'back-end' comes quickly in Yorkshire. At Michaelmas, 29th September, every farmhouse once looked forward to the stubble fattened Michaelmas goose. However, you needed two, because whether you liked it or not, tenant farmers were obliged to give a 'stubble' goose to their landlord when paying their rent on Michaelmas day.

Mischief Night, 4th November, was the night of the 'Plot' when a Yorkshireman, among others, attempted to blow up Parliament and King James I. Guy Fawkes was the son of a notary and educated at St Peter's School, York, who rather decently still refuse to burn the effigy of an 'old boy'. He was caught in the cellars of the Houses of Parliament with 36 barrels of gunpowder, and he met a horrible end. In Yorkshire on this night children played tricks, knocking on doors and running away, locking someone in the outside privy, or taking the garden gate off its hinges and '*chumpin*' for wood for the bonfire – all low grade naughtiness compared with nowadays

Food always tastes so good in the crisp night air, with the smell of wood smoke and flames from the bonfire. There are meat pies and mushy peas, jacket potatoes, and ginger biscuits to savour, but anyone with expensive dental work should steer clear of the traditional November 5th treats like chewy Parkin and sticky Plot Toffee.

Parkin

6 ozs flour
3 ozs each of brown sugar and butter
2 ozs oatmeal
4 ozs golden syrup
1 egg
1½ teaspoons bicarbonate of soda
1 teaspoon ground ginger
milk

Sift the dry ingredients into a bowl. Melt the sugar, syrup and butter and pour over the dry ingredients. Add the milk to make a soft consistency. Pour into a well greased tin. Bake for one hour in a medium to low oven.

If she was tired and had a quick nap or a cup of tea, my Yorkshire mother-in-law always said afterwards that she had 'come again like Parkin', meaning she was quite revived. The expression referred to the keeping properties of Parkin and how it is even better when eaten on the second or third day after baking.

Throughout the year food and drink was given and received; there was never a month without a celebration of some kind. What could be a more fitting tribute to generous hospitality than this, from a Yorkshire Farmers' Club after an annual dinner in 1847: 'The repast combined all the delicacies of the season and served up in the host's usual liberal manner'.

COOKING THE GOOSE

I wish you a merry Christmas
And a happy New Year.
A purse full o' money
An' a barrel full o' beer,
A good fat pig
That'll serve you through t' year,
An' please will you gi' me
My Christmas box.

A Christmas morning 'waits' song

Whatever hardships you endured through the year and however few or homely your presents, the one thing a Yorkshire mother tried to have was special food at Christmas. For those not living in town slums who could afford it, a Yorkshire Christmas was two days of intense eating, with someone doing the heavy duty cooking. The way Bradford writer William Cudworth in his *Owd Crismas Time* of 1906 put it, resonates with me even now: '*T' day before Crismas mi mother wor as fierce as a buck-ferrit, fettling up, an bakin' an getting all reddy for t' next day ...*' So no change there, then.

In the East Riding on Christmas Eve the church bells at 6 pm signalled the end of work. Summoned home by the 'frumenty bell', we can imagine the cold evening air and the warmth of Christmas smells as you opened the door: baked mince pies, freshly cut greenery and gently simmering frumenty. There are various spellings but they all come from the Latin *frumentum*, meaning corn.

Christmas Eve Frumenty
8 ozs 'kibbled' wheat
(wheat pounded roughly with a pestle and mortar)
3 pints water
¼ teaspoon salt

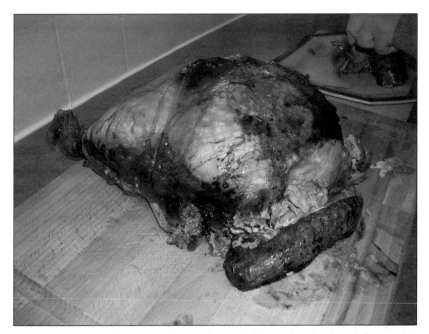

The Lewis family Christmas dinner of a Yorkshire turkey 'pot'. It fed seven big eaters, with plenty left over for the next day.

Wash and soak the wheat in water for one hour. Put into a stew pot with fresh water and salt. Add a nut of butter, mixed spice, currants, sugar, cream and rum to taste. Cook gently in a moderate oven until soft.

It is the nearest thing to eating a liquid spiced loaf. A similar dish, *fluffin,* used barley instead of wheat. Often the frumenty or *fluffin* was eaten as part of the ritual of the yule log. This was deeply significant ensuring a hearth and home that would never be cold. The log was brought in on Christmas Eve and laid on the fire, the lights were put out, and the oldest and youngest in the room or the head of the house lit candles from the yule log flame. The frumenty was served and eaten in silence, with the candles and log fire throwing shadows round the room.

You might be joined by friends and neighbours, or anyone you had done business with over the year for a Christmas 'pot'. It was very often the local feed and seed merchant who had supplied the wheat and candles as a present to the farm. Together you enjoyed mulled ale, frumenty, apple pie and soft white Wensleydale cheese. Pride of place was a giant gingerbread, weighing 6 lbs or more, which was never cut before Christmas Eve.

Pepper cake was another version of gingerbread, but with allspice or powdered cloves, and a slice was given to children when they called round at Christmas.

A little bit of pepper cake
A little bit of cheese.
A cup of cold water
And a penny, if you please.

The Christmas Eve mince pies have evolved from their original combined sweet and savoury mixture of minced beef or mutton, with raisins, currants and spices. The Victorians preferred their mince pies sweet, and now only suet represents the savoury element. Up until the 1940s suet could be obtained from several sources: minced cow's udder or in the dales minced pig's ear. I would have found a mince pie hard to enjoy then. The pastry case was once different too, a boat shape to represent the Bethlehem crib.

Another dish now lost to us is Christmas plum porridge, served for breakfast on Christmas morning in the grander Yorkshire houses. It was a bizarre mixture of beef or mutton broth, thickened with brown bread, together with raisins, currants and spices. Mercifully this fell out of favour, to be replaced by the dessert plum pudding we know and love today.

A good Yorkshire woman made the Yule or Christmas cake months in advance to let it mature. On the other hand the Christmas pudding was traditionally made on 'stir up Sunday', the nearest to St Andrew's Day (30th November). The Collect for that day exhorts: 'Stir up, we beseech Thee Lord, the wills of thy faithful people ...'. No Christmas pudding was complete without silver threepenny bits or little trinkets, like a thimble or a ring, hidden in its fruity depths. If you found the thimble in your pudding you were destined to remain single, but the ring foretold a wedding. Now we are warned of the dangers of accidentally swallowing such items, but does anyone remember such a thing happening? Having steamed gently in the washhouse the set pot for a couple of hours, the pudding was brought forth hot, with flaming brandy, the sprig of holly on top burnt to a crisp.

> *Ha well aw remember that big Christmas puddin.*
> *That puddin mooast famous of all in a year;*
> *When each lad at th' table mud stuff all he could in,*
> *And ne'er have a word of refusal to fear.*
> *Ha its raand speckled face, craand wi' sprigs o' green holly*
> *Seem'd sweeatin wi' juices of currants an' plums,*
> *An its fat cheeks made ivvery one laugh an feel jolly*
> *For it seem'd like a meetin' of long parted chums,*
> *That big Christmas puddin, that rich steeamin' puddin,*
> *That scrumptious plum puddin, mi mother had made.'*

John Hartley (1839–1915) born in Halifax and a
West Riding dialect writer

Once upon a Christmastime there was a prince amongst pies, a pie so glorious that we shall not see its like again. Though it is often written about, we lack the skill and digestion now for such a pie. The Yorkshire Christmas pye to be found in the 1778 edition of *The Frugal Housekeeper or the Compleat Cook: being the newest Collection of the most Genteel and least expensive* was neither frugal, genteel or inexpensive.

'To Make a Yorkshire Christmas Pye 1778.

First make a good standing crust, let the wall and bottom be very thick; bone a turkey, a goose, a fowl, a partridge, and a pigeon; season them all very well, take half an ounce of mace, half an ounce of nutmegs, a quarter of an ounce of cloves and a half an ounce of black pepper, all beat finely together, two large spoonfuls of salt and then mix them together: open the fowls down the back, and bone them, first the pigeon, then the partridge, cover them, then the fowl, then the goose and then the turkey, which must be large, season them well and lay them in the crust, so as it will look only like a whole turkey, then have a hare ready cased, and wiped with a clean cloth, cut it to pieces, that is joint it; season it, and lay it as close as you can on one side, on the other side woodcocks, moor game, and what sort of wild fowl you can get; season them well and lay them close, put at least four pounds of butter in the pye, then lay on your lid, which must be a very thick one and let it be well baked. It must be a very hot oven and it will take at least 4 hours. The crust will take a bushel of flour.

These pyes are often sent to London in a box as presents therefore the walls must be well built.'

A later version (1827) of a Yorkshire goose pie from *Domestic Economy and Cookery for Rich and Poor* by '*A Lady*' suggested stuffing the goose with a rich mixture of ox and calves tongues, 'or any number of smaller tongue', together with oysters and mushrooms. We must assume these gargantuan pies were available only to the rich and, together with the pigeons, pheasants, venison and hare caught on the country estates, were eaten up at the 'big house'. The gentry undoubtedly enjoyed and probably suffered from a surfeit of rich Christmas food.

Yet even now in Yorkshire the days of extravagant boning and stuffing have not passed altogether. There is still a butcher, probably more than one, who will prepare the more easily digested *Yorkshire Pots*. Derek Fox, a family butcher in Malton prepares and sells the nearest we shall ever come to tasting the gastronomic delights of previous centuries. Ready prepared and needing five hours' cooking, this magnificent Turkey Pot contains 'boned out game birds stuffed inside each other with various stuffings around each bird. Game may vary with each pot made, but the usual ones are turkey, chicken, pheasant, partridge, venison, livers from birds and pâté.' I spoke to the great butcher himself and inspected one he had made earlier, but he could not enlighten me as to the name 'pot'.

Anyone who cooks a Christmas goose now will buy it ready prepared. Few of us feel able to kill the goose first and, if asked to do so, would decide instantly to do without and just have more Brussels sprouts. Once if you wanted goose, more often than not you had the unpleasant business of killing it first. I heard the story of one grandfather, a farmer in West Witton, who, after catching his goose and bringing it inside, sat on a chair by the kitchen fire with the goose on his lap. Gently stroking the goose, the bird became comfortable and calm – who knows what its last thoughts were, perhaps, 'This is a nice place'. Grandfather then quietly slit

Fat geese in January: the ones that got away. (Photograph by Sylvia Turner)

its throat with a sharp knife and bled the bird over a bucket at his feet. The bird never struggled at any time and the meat was white and tender.

In 37 years of marriage I have cooked a Christmas goose only once and it will never happen again. A veil should be drawn over the whole sorry business, but all I will say is that, what with the basting, constant draining of fat and some indifferent meat at the end of it, I was far removed from any Christmas spirit.

You cannot cook just any old goose, and whether it will be tender and succulent depends on the age of the bird. There was a newly married young woman cooking her first Christmas dinner. She was given, generously she thought, an old goose, plucked and prepared by the Yorkshire farmer where her husband worked. She consulted her old neighbour on how best to cook this goose, who advised: 'First get an old house brick and soak it in cold water for two hours. Put the goose at the top of the oven and the wet brick at the bottom. Roast slowly for two hours, draining the fat whenever it looks like spilling over onto the brick below. Cook for another hour on a high heat, and remember to keep basting the goose. When cooked allow to rest for 20 minutes. Warm a serving dish and place the brick on the serving dish; take the goose, and throw it in the dustbin!'

If goose was not an option, you did your best with 'poor man's goose', which was either pig's or lamb's heart and liver layered in a pie with onions and potatoes and perhaps a bit of bacon. A joint of pickled beef, pork or jugged hare were all thought a worthy Christmas dinner, but roasted rabbit on Christmas Day meant times were hard.

A small cookery book published by the *Northern Echo* in 1912 assured its readers that 'The *Northern Echo* Devotes Special Attention to matters of interest to Lady Readers.' In this case it was giblet pie.

> 'This is a handy dish for Christmas when there is so much poultry about. Take giblets from turkey or goose, or two sets of fowls, wash them and take gall from liver, cut heart in two, pick the head, remove the eyes, and chop off beak. Skin feet and gizzard, cut feet in two, neck and gizzard in four.'

After this feat of butchery, you simply simmered the above with onions, parsley and thyme for two hours and then added some previously stewed steak and two hard boiled eggs, and topped with short crust pastry and baked. I hope it was worth the effort.

Until the early 1960s a bought chicken was expensive, but at the same time as chicken became cheaper so too did the ubiquitous turkey. What is it about the intensity of the taste of food we remember from childhood? It leaves us with a lingering grown-up disappointment that somehow food is not the same any more; I feel that way about turkey. We owe the arrival of the turkey in this country to a Yorkshire man. It is said that William Strickland of Boynton Hall, near Bridlington, introduced the birds on his return from America, where he had travelled with Jean Cabot, the Genoese navigator, in the 1500s. An old saying claimed:

> *Hops, turkeys, carp and beer,*
> *Came into England all in one year.*

Something that has surprised me researching this book is how everyone seemed so sociable. Nowadays we try and see family at Christmas, but in the past the wider community celebrated together and it was the chapel which provided the focus for glorious teas and celebrations. 'A tea festival was held in Keld Congregational Chapel on Christmas Day at which upwards of 360 partook' – a simple announcement but who was doing the cooking? We know the answer, for somehow the women of this small community in Swaledale found the time and energy to fit in extra baking around Christmas. Few of us would offer now.

I have already written of the monotonous diet of the workhouse, and at Christmas the bleakness and desolation of one's circumstances must have been hard to bear. We all know the opening lines of the famous Victorian monologue 'Christmas Day in the Workhouse' by George Sims, which, when recited by a whiskered gentlemen in a warm parlour after a good dinner and a glass of port, never failed to bring a tear to the eye:

'It is Christmas Day in the workhouse
And the cold bare walls are bright
With garlands of green and holly,
And the place is a pleasant sight:
For with clean-washed hands and faces,
In a long and hungry line
The paupers sit at the tables,
For this is the hour they dine.'

It goes on to tell how one old man refuses the pudding and blames the Board of Guardians for not helping his wife, who had died the previous Christmas. Yet in some well-run workhouses, just for a couple of days, kindness and charity went hand in hand. The *Wensleydale Advertiser* of 1847 reported another kind of Christmas Day in a workhouse:

'On Christmas Day the inmates of the Union Workhouse received their customary treat. A plentiful dinner provided, consisting of the staple fare of England: the

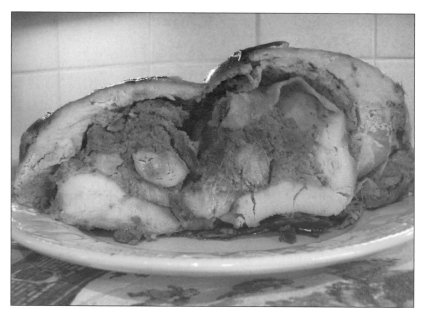

Boxing Day and a section showing the full meaty glories inside the Yorkshire turkey 'pot' of boned chicken, pheasant, partridge, venison, livers and pâté, and even then there was some left over.

paupers sat down to excellent roast beef, plum pudding and all the usual accompaniments to those national viands. After dinner the governor, Mr R.O. Warwick, R.N., proposed the health of the Chairman and the Board of Guardians, with thanks to them and the other kind friends whose liberality provided the banquet... In the evening all inmates partook of a good tea, with plenty of plum cake. A similar treat was given on New Year's day, and on both occasions St George's flag was hoisted, as is usual on joyous anniversaries.'

This was not just an example of the generosity of a country and farming community, because in 1860 the ladies and gentlemen on the Leeds Board of Guardians of the new workhouse in Burmantofts were no less generous. Nearly 500 men and women sat down to a Christmas dinner of roast beef and plum pudding, followed by coffee. 'By the hearty appetites of the diners they were disposed of 46 stones of beef, 6 of suet, 37 of potatoes, and the pudding contained 100 lbs of plums, 50 lbs of currants, 40 lbs of sultanas. Sweets and tobacco came afterwards and an entertainment of a free and easy character ended the day.'

High up, out of sight in the corner of our utility room, hangs a bunch of brown wizened twigs with something black stuck to the stems. I do not allow many people into this inner sanctum, for close inspection of this dead decoration would reveal that it is last year's mistletoe. This in our house is the symbol of Twelfth Night. Forget the wassail bowl, feasts, games and plays of medieval England, for most of us Twelfth Night is simply when you take down your decorations. Ray's mother in Leeds always kept the mistletoe for a year and my rational, sensible Yorkshire husband insists on doing the same, as he firmly believes the rhyme she taught him:

With mistletoe over your head,
You'll never want for bread.

KEEPING JOLLY

'And in the morning when they did awake,
They curst and swore that all their heads did ake;
O York-shire, York-shire! Thy ale it is so strong,
That it will kill us all if we stay long.'

From The Praise of Yorkshire Ale, *1697*

Beer has been around since 6,000 BC. The Book of Genesis in the Old Testament mentions wine: Noah planted a vineyard, got very drunk, and caused a lot of family problems. Which just goes to show there is often trouble with 'keeping jolly'. As Dr Johnson famously said: 'Wine makes a man better pleased with himself … But the danger is, that while a man grows better pleased with himself, he may be growing less pleasing to others.' Sadly, in Yorkshire, as in so many other counties, many succumbed to the demon drink. Until the 18th century only the very young and invalids drank milk; the rest of the population enjoyed beer or water. Water was the dangerous option, as in towns most water supplies were heavily polluted with effluent from countless privies, sewers and middens.

The occupants of large country houses drank beer from their own brewhouse but, at the other end of the social scale, the common alehouse was a room in the home of the person who brewed the ale, and it was here that the poor hung out. Taverns in towns were superior and sold wine for a better class of person: professional gentlemen, lawyers, doctors and affluent tradesmen, who discussed business whilst drinking and eating. Not unnaturally, people with money attracted an assortment of 'loose' women and fraudsters. Political drinking clubs were popular, and in Hull the local Whigs met in 'mug houses' for political discussion and ale, 'which sometimes is Drunk to suche a Pitch that th' Remarks they make about one another would be better to have remain'd a Secret'.

THE ANGEL INN, FERRYBRIDGE.

Coaching Inns on the Great North Road. (From The Old Coaching Days in Yorkshire *by Tom Bradley, published in 1889)*

THE GEORGE INN, CATTERICK BRIDGE.

In addition to these drinking establishments, the old coaching inns were a melting pot for travellers needing refreshment. Up and down the Great North Road, from Bawtry in the south going north through Doncaster, Wentbridge, Ferrybridge, Boroughbridge, Catterick Bridge and on to Scotch Corner, the song of the 'Three Jolly Postboys' rang out:

> *'Landlord fill the bowl till it does flow over,*
> *For there's not a jolly soul that goes to bed sober.*
> *He that drinks and goes to bed sober,*
> *Falls as the leaves fall and dies in October.*
> *He that drinks and goes to bed mellow,*
> *Lives as he ought to live, and dies a jolly fellow.'*

Before commercial brewing captured the market, women brewed at home, sharing the items needed for the brewing process, as few could afford all the utensils. Malt, hops and yeast were bought, but often yeast was given to be paid back when you next brewed. 'Persons sometimes spend many hours in seeking yeast to brew or bake with. If they seek it in their own locality it is to borrow, if outside it is to buy. There is public house yeast but most people prefer home-brewed yeast to it,' according to Joseph Lawson, writing in his book *Progress in Pudsey* in 1887, but living in the safety of Horsforth. The people of Pudsey also preferred their own beer as it was free from 'the pernicious adulterations most of the ales and porters are subject to'. A *mugpot* of home-brewed beer was always available, and everyone believed it to be a

Sign outside Tan Hill, the highest pub in England at 1,732 feet, and a favourite refreshment stop on the Pennine Way.

most nourishing drink, especially with an oatcake dipped in it. Children were encouraged 'to open their shoulders, and let it go down'.

With the growth of industrialisation, public houses sprang up in every market square, street, corner and alleyway. The alehouses ceased to brew their own supplies, and commercial brewers made new fortunes supplying the public houses. Some great Yorkshire brewery names like Theakston of Masham remain independent, but most are now swallowed up in multinational companies. Samuel Smith's brewery started in 1758 in Tadcaster, where the well water from the limestone strata was particularly good. In the 1840s, two brothers, John and Sam Smith, divided the business between them; their names live on. Joshua Tetley started brewing in Leeds in 1822, and Timothy Taylor in Keighley in 1858, taking advantage of the Pennine spring water.

A feature of Yorkshire life from the 1700s onwards was that every town and decent sized village had its own brewery.

> 'we've ale that's strong and old,
> Both from North-Allerton and Easingwold;
> From Sutton, Thirske ...
> Wee've ale also that's call'd Knocker-down.'

The complete history of brewing in Yorkshire would take a book of its own, but I will give just one example of the wealth to be made from brewing and the growth of the public house. The earliest commercial brewer in Wakefield, in the 1700s, was Robert Harrison. In 1794, describing himself as 'late common brewer', he possessed land, a small fortune of £1,400 in cash, and a well furnished house. By 1870 there were 107 inns, taverns and hotels in Wakefield, all of which relied on supplies from Yorkshire commercial brewers. Drink was everywhere and fortunes were there for the making.

Men were not just drinking in their spare time. Sheffield and Barnsley were once great brewing centres catering for the workers in the steel-making and heavy metalworking industries. The heat meant that the men needed constantly to replace the liquid lost in sweat by regular trips to the nearest public house. At Kirkstall Forge, on the banks of the river Aire in Leeds, the management offered beer. Old records show a labourer working in a forge earned '1s 4d a day with two drinkings. The brewing was done by one of the carters, called John Blackburn, and in 1803 they brewed 47 times and 34 times in 1804'.

My favourite 'tipple' gin caused many a downfall. Popularly referred to as 'mother's ruin', it was invented by a Dutch professor of medicine who distilled maize, malt and rye with juniper berries. It was cheap and, drunk in large quantities, it deadened the reality of a squalid, wretched life. It was given to babies in their bottles to keep them quiet, used as an abortifacient, and caused untold misery and death. Today's young people may think they have invented 'binge drinking' and that Saturday nights are for lying senseless in a pool of vomit, but the reality of the 1700s and 1800s was far worse.

The problems caused by drink – wasted money that should have gone on food, ill health, brutality and domestic violence – were all cause for concern amongst social reformers. Joseph Lawson painted a grim picture of Yorkshire cotton and woollen workers in *Progress in Pudsey*: 'Christmas was both a merry and yet a sad time – there being so much drunkenness'. But he went on,

> 'However bad Pudsey might be at that time, Yeadon was much worse, and had a large number of reckless and low characters in proportion to its population. Very little work was done on Mondays, and its public-houses were generally crowded with drunken men, pugilists and their backers. Very little work was done from Saturday to Tuesday by a large number.'

It would be easy to think that I had singled out industrial Yorkshire as an example of the drunkenness to be seen on any street corner and that sobriety and decency ruled in the countryside. Not so, for market day in the country towns was a nightmare of drunken farmers, able to get home only because the horse knew the way. Walter White wrote in *A Month in Yorkshire* (1861), a description of life in Wensleydale that we can only be thankful we will never have to witness:

> 'Aysgarth – a tall maypole stands on the green ... It is a

memorial of the sports and pastimes for which Wensleydale is famous. The annual feast and fairs would attract visitors from 20 miles around. Here, at Aysgarth, not the least popular part of the amusements were the races run by men stark naked, as people not more than 40 years old can well remember. But times are changed and throughout the dale drunkenness and revelry are giving place to teetotalisim, lectures, tea gatherings and other moral recreations.'

The temperance movement was an attractive option for those wanting a better life. To start with, moderation in drinking was the aim – no spirits, just beer and wine – but this swiftly moved to complete abstinence. By 1829 the temperance movement in Belfast had spread through Ireland, into Scotland and then to England, where in 1832 a group of working men in Preston signed a pledge that they would never again drink alcohol. At first the whole idea of doing without alcohol was seen as odd and suspicious, as Joseph Lawson reported:

'When Teetotalism first came up, the few who happened to be its first adherents and propagators were mostly persons of somewhat pale countenance, and the great proof of health at that day was ruddy complexion and robustness. We really thought they were carrying the thing too far.'

The Anglicans and the Nonconformists were part of the revolt against drink, with Methodists, Baptists, Quakers and later the Salvation Army leading the way. They were successful in lobbying for limiting public house opening hours and one wonders what those campaigners would make of our current legislation on 24-hour drinking – spinning in their graves probably. Temperance clubs and societies were founded for education and also served as an alcohol-free place where the working man could socialize, read the newspapers, and play draughts and dominoes. Two Yorkshire men spotted a market opportunity for non-alcoholic drink, and in 1871 Ben Shaw and his brother started 'Shaw Brothers,

Manufacturers of Non-alcoholic Beverages' in Huddersfield, making organic beverages like horehound beer, botanic porter and dandelion stout for the working man to enjoy.

Children, too, needed to be educated in the evils of alcohol, and in 1847 the Band of Hope was formed for working class children in Leeds. Children joined from the age of six and made a pledge of total abstinence. In return there were social activities, choirs and organized outings. A child from a poor home would have needed little persuasion.

Tea festivals were popular and an occasion to spread the message:

> 'A Public Temperance Tea Festival will be held in Hawes on Thursday June 17th 1847 at 3 o' clock in the afternoon, the members of the Association will form its procession and perambulate the street, headed by the Hawes Teetotal Band and at 4 o' clock, Tea (provided in a spacious Marquee, opposite Mr Whitley's Coffee House) will be on the Table: in the evening, the Celebrated Champion in the Cause of Temperance, Dr F.R. Lees, F.S.A., Edin., will deliver a Lecture on Food or Famine; the Accordance of Teetotalism with the arrangements of Nature; the Uses and Adaptations of Food and Drink; the Manufacture and Consumption of Alcoholic Beverages, a complete Subversion of those Uses and Arrangements, and a Breach of Divine Law; the national Waste Incurred and its Evil Effects on the Moral, Political, and Physical Condition of the People. Tickets of Admission for the Tea, 6d each.'

Strong words indeed.

What bliss it must have been to live in Saltaire. In 1853 Sir Titus Salt, a manufacturer of worsted cloth, built the largest factory in the world, together with decent houses, schools, a Congregational church and a hospital for his workers. A medical report of 1867 wrote glowingly:

> 'There is no public house in Saltaire. Thus, with comfortable houses and every inducement to stay at home – with literary and social institutions in their very

midst, with high-class tastes, and, to crown all, a beautiful temple to the worship of God – it would be strange indeed had Saltaire not a reputation and a name.'

In the late 1600s coffee was imported from Turkey, chocolate from the West Indies and South America, and tea came overland from China across Asia – and it was all expensive. York was not slow to follow London and Oxford with Parkers Coffee House opening in the Minster Yard in 1697, followed by one in Leeds a year later. Coffee and chocolate were drunk, mainly by professional men. The new Coffee House in Scarborough kept the riff-raff out by charging a subscription, for which you could have use of pen, paper and ink. It was only when the East India Company set up tea plantations in India and shipped it back to Britain in the fast tea-clippers that the poor got a look in with a cup of tea.

Coffee drinking was macho, but tea was for ladies, and upper class ladies at that, who kept the tea caddy locked against thieving servants. After each brew the tea was dried out, saved and passed down through the servant hierarchy, until sold at the back door to outsiders. Sadly by then the tea was exhausted of any taste and so dried leaves from a sloe or blackcurrant bush were added to give some bulk and a pinch of bicarbonate of soda as a 'livener'. What must it have been like to drink?

Which may explain the success of Charles Taylor and his quality Yorkshire Tea. He had been the northern agent for a London tea company and he knew that local variations in water could affect the quality of a brew. So in 1886 he founded Taylors of Harrogate and, through diligence and attention to detail, made the most suitable blend of tea for each area in Yorkshire. The company prospered and grew from being simply a regional wholesaler to owning a chain of coffee shops, known as 'The Kiosks'.

In the 1960s, Taylors joined forces with its friendly rival, Bettys Café Tea Rooms, and Bettys was awarded the first ever Tea Council 'Top Tea Place of the Year' award in recognition of the range and quality of teas, all supplied by Taylors. Many do not consider a visit to Harrogate, Ilkley, York or Northallerton to be complete without the pleasure of a trip to Bettys for some welcoming hospitality and a civilised cup of tea.

Today, 9 million cups of Yorkshire Tea are enjoyed across the UK every single day. (By kind permission of Bettys and Taylors of Harrogate)

However, all this was in the future. The great explosion of tea drinking among the poor met with a mixed reception from the social reformers: educated people who thought it a sinister development. William Cobbett, the journalist and radical politician, wrote many worthy pamphlets highlighting the plight

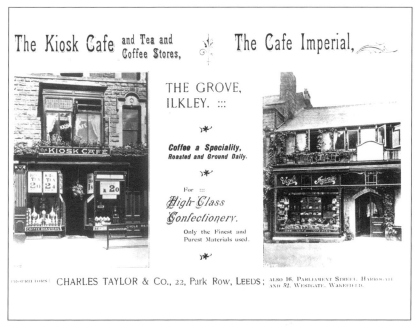

The Kiosk Cafe and Tea and Coffee Stores,   The Cafe Imperial,

THE GROVE,
ILKLEY. :::

)*'

Coffee a Speciality,
Roasted and Ground Daily.

)*'

For :::

High-Class
Confectionery.

Only the Finest and
Purest Materials used.

)*'

PROPRIETORS: CHARLES TAYLOR & CO., 22, Park Row, LEEDS; ALSO 16, PARLIAMENT STREET, HARROGATE AND 52, WESTGATE, WAKEFIELD.

Fashionable Ilkley 1900. 'The Kiosk' is now Bettys Café Tea Rooms. As well as Charles Taylor's success at blending tea, the company opened a chain of coffee shops known as 'The Kiosks', where coffee was freshly roasted in the shop window. (By kind permission of Bettys and Taylors of Harrogate)

of the poor, but 'The Vice of Tea Drinking' was not one of them. The all male clergy feared women would be idle if not busy making beer. A similar worry was that, as tea was so easily made, women would substitute a cup of tea for breakfast instead of cooking porridge for their family.

A doctor in Otley regarded tea as 'evil' and 'particularly hurtful to the female constitution'. Other medical men worried about the nutritional content of tea as opposed to beer, which they thought better for you. A cup of hot sweet tea has little nutrition but it temporarily warmed and offered some comfort to the poor and hungry. Any left over in the pot was warmed up again at bedtime with a drop more milk and poured onto some bread with a sprinkle of sugar. This was known as 'tea boily', and you were either very poor or very thrifty, but at least you went to bed feeling full.

Enjoying tea in the Valley Gardens, Harrogate, an Edwardian summer pastime. (By kind permission of Bettys Café Tearoom, Harrogate)

In spite of the temperance movement, one activity remained constant, for there is no greater sin in Yorkshire than waste. With free ingredients in the fields and hedgerows, who was not going to make a drop of home-made wine, purely for medicinal purposes, of course. Home-made wines vary in taste and potency, as many have discovered on being invited to taste a drop and finding their legs go from under them. Yet committed teetotallers took a glass 'to keep the cold out' and the local Methodist minister would take a drop of home-made wine when he visited.

Margaret Hopper was a remarkable Dales personality and stalwart of the Women's Institute who did much during the Second World War and afterwards to make people aware of the traditional food and drink of Yorkshire. She was an expert cheese-maker and educated Yorkshire women in skills which, with the advent of convenience food, they were rapidly losing. Her 1951 pamphlet 'Hedgerow Harvest', published for the Festival of Britain, gave clear instructions on how to make wine at any time of the year.

Making sloe gin. Half fill a clean jar with sloes, which have been pricked all over with a fork, and then add sugar – the amount depends on how sweet you like it, but too much and it tastes like cough medicine. Fill to the top with gin and cover. Give the jar a good shake every day, and it will be ready by Christmas. Strain through fine muslin. Enjoy the ruby rich colour and warming glow on a cold winter's night.

Normally rhubarb wine was made with the second growth in August, but this canny lady worked on the principal of 'a bird in the hand', and advised on making it in the spring in case a dry summer meant no second growth. Other delightful fermentations were orange wine and an interesting home-made hock. The summer months produced wines from cherries, gooseberries, raspberries, loganberries, black and red currants. In late summer, children picked hedgerow blackberries and elderberries for the inevitable elderberry wine, which in my childhood meant exploding bottles and purple froth spilling down the larder walls.

In autumn there was apple wine from the windfalls, and wine

Elderberry cordial is good for colds. Gather ripe berries on a dry day and put them into jars, having first removed the stalks. Stand the jars in boiling water until the juice runs. Strain off the juice and to every quart add 1 ounce of bruised ginger, 1 teaspoon of cloves and 2 lbs of sugar. Simmer gently for an hour, leave until cold, strain and bottle. Easier and less messy, in my opinion, than elderberry wine.

from ripe grapes (or unripe in a bad season), plum and damson port, and home-made sherry, using potatoes, raisins and grapes. By winter you were onto vegetables such as potatoes for a cheeky raisin and potato wine, turnips and beetroot. Parsnip and ginger wine kept the Yorkshire cold out nicely, at the same time acting as a very efficacious purgative. We really were drinking for the benefit of our health.

Margaret Hopper's Parsnip Wine

8 lbs of parsnips
2 ozs bruised ginger
3½ lbs of brown sugar
1 oz of yeast
1 gallon of water

Scrub but do not peel the parsnips, and cut into small pieces. Bring to the boil in a pan with no lid and add the ginger. Boil for 30 minutes. Strain, add the sugar, and when cool add the yeast. Let it stand for 2 or 3 days and strain again. Bottle, adding a few raisins to each bottle. After a month add a little sugar to each bottle. Do not cork too tightly at first.

A visitor to Yorkshire on a walking holiday in the Dales went into a pub on a hot day and asked for something, long, cold and full of gin. The landlord replied, 'You can have the wife.'

FISH, FLESH AND GOOD RED HERRING

A dish fit for onny King
Is yan o' them ling pies,
Staithes women – an they're wise
Knows what ti deea wi' ling.

Staithes was once a lively fishing village cut off from the rest of the world; its curious isolation is now preserved for the tourists. The writer of a Ward Lock 1939 guide book thought it 'one of the quaintest places in the kingdom. The men are an honest, stalwart race, whose most apparent fault is a propensity for letting their equally stalwart womenfolk do the major share of whatever work may be going. In the cod-fishing season, it is amusing to watch the short skirted women dragging great codfish about, holding the slippery creature by the gills'.

The isolation meant much intermarriage in the village, and any girl coming from the outside would not have been brought up to the work. Staithes women were tough and, when not landing the catches, hauling up cobles, baiting lines with hundreds of mussels, looking after family and home, they were expected to cook a good *ling* pie. Ling is a species of cod with solid meat and looks like a short conger eel; woof is a kind of catfish caught off the Yorkshire coast. Staithes was noted for ling pie and Scarborough for woof pie.

Ling or Woof Pie

Boil or steam some ling or woof and remove the flesh from the bones and skin. Season with salt and pepper and sprinkle with a little flour. Cut some lean, uncooked bacon into pieces. Slice some hardboiled eggs. Finely chop a small onion. Place fish, bacon, eggs and onion in layers in a

Girls skaning mussels in the 1890s at Tate Hill, on the east side of Whitby. Mussels were used as bait for the long lines, and it was the women's job to collect, open and take out (skane) the mussels and bait the lines for the fishermen going out to sea. There were 200 hooks per line and a normal boat had 12 lines. (Photograph by Frank Meadow Sutcliffe. By kind permission of The Sutcliffe Gallery, Whitby)

Nelly Backhouse (second from left) owned this fish stall situated on the New Quay at Whitby. (Photograph taken circa 1890 by Frank Meadow Sutcliffe. By kind permission of The Sutcliffe Gallery, Whitby)

greased pie dish and pour on ½ pint of milk. Top with shortcrust pastry and cook in a moderately hot oven for about an hour.

This is the standard cookery book recipe but, according to a more authentic version still cooked by families with their roots in the fishing industry, the middle section of the ling is put in an ovenproof dish with pieces of bacon on top, sliced onions and potatoes at the side, a little water to moisten, and a pastry crust on top.

Eventually the Staithes fishermen moved to Whitby, although herring was still caught from Staithes in the 1900s. In the boom years of the 1880s there were more than 200 boats fishing in the herring season, from July to September, and the herring industry was important on the north-east coast up until the 1950s. The herrings were preserved by salting and were sealed in barrels for selling on or kippered in smoke houses over smouldering oak wood chips. People still remember buying a bucket of fresh herrings for 6d.

Everything I know about fishing I learned from one man – Tom Roe – who once fished off both Staithes and Whitby. Lobster is potted closer in shore, and crabs in deeper water. Lobsters were sent to Staithes, where a dealer bought them, or they were auctioned at Whitby fish market. I think of lobster and crab as luxury food but on the east coast you could eat them every day. When fishing, Tom recalled that for every twelve lobsters you caught four crabs. He would let his friend take the crabs home, as Tom's mother made crab sandwiches for his midday 'bait'; then, on going home, there was crab salad for tea and finally at suppertime, more crab. Not unnaturally he grew sick of it. As a married man he always kept a lobster back, because if he did not there would have been hell to pay from the cat, who had been brought up on it. At times Tom's family sat down to a meal of six lobsters and four or five crabs.

I came across a wartime recipe for traditional Whitby mock crab, which did not contain a shred of crab. Skinned tomatoes were mixed with butter, breadcrumbs, salt and pepper and cooked for a short time; then cheese was added and finally an egg. Alright for humans in times of austerity, but definitely not good enough for Tom's cat.

A fish enjoyed by Tom was 'tangle cod', caught in the seaweed and richly coloured bright red to brown from the iodine in the seaweed. The meat was good and firm from the pounding of the breaking waves, as opposed to the floppy flesh of the deep sea cod, but the fishermen did not sell it as they never caught enough. Tom cut the head off and boiled it for that cat – was there ever such a pampered creature – then rubbed in a good covering of salt, nicked the tail and hung it for 24 hours. It was then ready to bake, and the meat was delicious, 'fluffy and flaky, with white sauce and mashed potatoes'.

Tom recalled happy summer days taking a boat, a picnic and a bucket to the Kettle Ness end of Runswick Bay. While the children played and collected driftwood for a fire, Tom scraped limpets off the rocks with a sharp knife then boiled them in a bucket over the fire for about 10 minutes. They tasted salty and not unlike chewing a lump of leather but not too bad with a loaf of bread.

They were a doughty lot of women over on the east coast. Tom's granny, Ethel Dohring, made a living from what we would call today 'outside catering'. She lived in Skinningrove on the coast and cooked pasties for the miners and those working in the iron and steel works. Every morning she turned out pasties made of layers of potatoes, thin slices of beef, onion, and more potatoes, all encased in pastry. The pasties were wrapped in clean tea towels when they came out of the oven, to keep them moist, and the men bought them on their way to work. The next day they were there again for more, but always brought the tea towels back for washing. Then at lunchtime she was down in the village selling her homemade pork pies and, in the evening, fried fish and chips from a coal-fired chip pan from the back of a horse-drawn trailer. When did this woman sleep?

I have never eaten a gull's egg, so cannot write from experience. I am told that they have a distinctive salty, fish flavour and a dark reddish yellow yolk, and they made an interesting Yorkshire pudding. They were also used for baking, or you had them boiled. It was possible to buy these eggs in the 1930s from a basket outside a shop in Church Street, Whitby. The Bird Protection Act in 1954 made taking wild bird eggs illegal but before then Yorkshire men saw no reason not to risk life and limb collecting the eggs from seabirds, and the guillemot's eggs were much sought after.

Between Filey and Flamborough Head are the spectacular Bempton and Speeton Cliffs where, in spring, thousands of guillemots, razor-bills and kittiwakes nest on the cliffs. Farmers with fields adjacent to the cliffs had the right to gather eggs and they 'allowed' the farmhands and other local men to descend the 400-foot cliff-face between May and July to collect the eggs from the nesting birds. The 'climmers', with huge bags hung from either side of their bodies, collected up to 400 eggs on every descent. Some were sold locally but most were sent to London.

This activity closely resembled modern-day abseiling but with the egg collecting adding an extra hazard. It was only for the brave, although the description from a 1939 Ward Lock guide assured the reader it was impossible to fall out of the harness, 'even if the wearer becomes insensible'. It still required enormous strength and a good head for heights, though. 'In passing over the cliff edge, the climber walks backwards down the steep slope ... drives a small steel pulley with a spike attached into the earth or a crack in the rock. Over this he lays the rope which is attached to his body, and boldly leaning his full weight upon it, places his feet upon the rock and practically walks backwards down the face of the cliffs. The climber is held by one man only, who sits on the cliff top with his feet firmly planted in two holes dug for the purpose. This man wears round his waist a broad belt of strong padded leather round which the rope is passed, so that the weight falls upon the loins.'

With the eggs collected, the 'climmer' jerked on the rope to give the signal to two other men at the top, who then spent an exhausting five minutes hauling him up. A hard hat, often a bowler, was essential for protection from falling rock and the outraged birds.

Even inland the birds were not safe from the egg collectors. On the North Yorkshire Moors some ponds had smaller seabirds nesting and local lads enjoyed a day out collecting the eggs. People remember, as far inland as Wensleydale, egg collectors descending on Askrigg with big baskets to scramble up the hillside to a pond where the gulls nested. However, the birds had the last laugh: they moved their nests away from the edge of the pond and onto a small island in the centre where it was impossible to collect the eggs without getting soaked. Gulls 1 : Egg Collectors 0.

Swinging out. 'The further the descent is made, the greater the swinging motion, and the climber is frequently suspended in mid-air, many feet away from the cliff.' (From the Ward Lock Guide *of 1939)*

Beef was undoubtedly the meat for a treat. It would be eaten on Sundays, at family gatherings, and at celebrations – and, if you were a prosperous tradesman or a well paid artisan, during the week, too. People ate with gusto. 'Fingers were made afore forks. It's mebbe nut very genteel ti pick bones with yer teeth, but gentry losses a lot of sweet meat with their fine manners. Nearer the bone, sweeter the meat.' Even in the workhouse you had boiled beef on a Sunday, followed by endless beef broth from the bones.

Beef comes from castrated males, known as bullocks, and, although readers from farming stock will know this, it is important for those sanitized from the realities of farming to be enlightened. Cattle were driven down from Scotland along the old drovers' roads and sold at English markets to be fattened up on lowland grazing. These cattle ended up with the butcher and an old name for a row of butchers' shops was *shambles*, the most famous being in York, but the butchers are long gone.

Beef was salted and boiled, and with some ingenuity tough beef could be made to taste as good as hare.

Huddersfield Hare

Cut the beef into strips and sprinkle with black pepper, nutmeg and flour, and fry lightly. Place some celery, mushrooms, shredded parsnip and an onion stuck with cloves in a deep hare pot and put the strips of beef on top. Put the lid on tightly. Cook in a slow oven for two hours.

Beef dripping, once sieved and stored, produced exceptional ginger biscuits, and, according to my Yorkshire source, was the secret ingredient for winning prizes at produce shows; it enhanced the ginger flavour and had the judges salivating at the taste.

Yorkshire is not short of sheep, and those grazed on heather have a special taste. Sweet as young lambs might look, that does not stop many of us from eating them. Not all farmers are hard-hearted, and some, hating the soulful bleating of the mothers when the lambs are taken away, never eat lamb. Unlike the old Yorkshire farmer putting his sheep through the sheep dip as two visitors stopped to admire the flock: 'We do so like the smell of sheep,' they said and the old farmer replied, 'Yis an' seea deea ah, but ah leykes t' teeast on 'em better.'

The sheep is an economical beast: 'Of the sheep is cast away nothing,' for besides the leg, saddle and shoulder joints, there is the neck, breast, loin, chops, liver, kidneys and, of course, the sheep's

Yorkshire Dales lambs – it makes you think, doesn't it? (Photograph by Richard H. Fawcett)

head. There was little you could not do with a sheep's head – in a pie; baked; stuffed with savoury breadcrumbs; or turned into broth with a turnip, carrot, celery and barley – and the tongue was coated in flour and fried. The *Northern Echo* in 1912 gave its readers the recipe for 'How to Cook a Sheep's Head with Brain Sauce', but I shall spare you the details. Mint sauce and capers were the traditional accompaniment, but the herb samphire, an acquired taste, was gathered from the banks of the Humber, boiled and used as a vegetable for mutton.

Once, most Yorkshire people ate mutton, although there is a debate as to the exact definition of the term. Wensleydale butcher Harold Hammond defined it as meat from a ewe which has had at least one lamb, and that is good enough for me. The derogatory expression 'mutton dressed as lamb' for a woman who dresses to appear younger than her years fails to take into account that mutton cooked carefully and slowly can be very tasty. Like older women, mutton is overlooked now, but some top chefs are trying to bring it back with a 'mutton renaissance campaign' backed by Prince Charles.

Just like beef, the joint of lamb or mutton was a treat for Sunday … and for the rest of the week. 'Hot on Sunday, cold on

Monday, hashed on Tuesday, minced on Wednesday, curried Thursday, broth on Friday, cottage pie on Saturday.'

I have already mentioned William Cobbett and his pamphlets (page 74); he also had an interesting view of women. He wrote 'Advice to Young Men - Never you mind about the piece of needlework, the tambourine and the maps of the world made by her needle. Get to see her at work upon a mutton chop, or a bit of bread and cheese, and if she deal quickly with them, you have a pretty security for that activity, without which a wife is a burden instead of being a help.'

With beef or lamb, the butcher had done the killing and cutting up; there was never a relationship with the meat. Unlike that of the pig with a working class family: it might be a family pet but was always destined for the table. It was a special day when the pig was killed, with children helping and friends and neighbours all pitching in.

Pig-keeping was not just for the country. Many of the sanitary problems in Yorkshire towns arose from keeping a pig in your backyard. My sister-in-law remembered her father keeping a pig in Pontefract, but in more appropriate conditions on an allotment. The neighbours provided scraps of leftovers and in return they expected something from the pig. Children skipped and sang:

Dearly beloved brethren isn't it a sin,
When you peel potatoes to throw away the skin?
The skin will feed the pigs and the pigs will feed you,
Dearly beloved brethren isn't this true?'

The scraps were cooked in the set pot in the outhouse and for a hungry boy there was 'nothing better than a handful of pig taties straight out of the copper'.

During the Second World War pigs were registered and rationing applied. A person was fined if caught killing a pig for their own use, but that is not to say that in more remote places the odd pig didn't 'escape' documentation. Few of us could do now what was commonplace until the late 1940s. The family pig was killed in November, but never on a Friday, as this was unlucky. It was quite an occasion, and there was even a quick and easy 'Pig

Killing Cake', made from shortcrust pastry, currants and sugar, which was served hot with butter to the helpers.

What follows is a graphic description from Mr Ron Stephenson of Lythe, of pig killing in the 1940s, and I warn those of a delicate disposition that some of it is of a disturbing nature. Bear in mind a pig can weigh 20 stones; so this was very much a team effort. The pig was roped and stunned by hitting a mallet onto a 5-inch iron bolt placed on the pig's forehead. Another man stood by and had a knife ready to slit the pig's throat.

The blood was caught in a bowl, and here the children were useful, as it was their job to keep the warm blood moving with their hands, so that it would not coagulate and become lumpy. The blood was for black pudding, to be made next day with hot fat, barley and seasoning. The pig was placed on its side in a tub of very hot water, lined with a chain which was worked backwards and forwards to remove the bristles and then turned over to do the other side. 'Many of the men had scrapers for the bristles, some were made out of shoe polish tin lids and others had proper ones made by the blacksmith.' A *creel*, a kind of bench with wooden slats, was placed at the side of the tub and the pig lifted on and the men finished taking the bristles off.

> 'One chap would have a hand hook and he would pull off the claws, the main man would trim the ears (lugs) up. Then cold water would be tipped over the pig and the pig would be turned over. Main man would use a knife to cut into the legs and take out the tendons. Two or four men (depending on the size of the pig) would cart the pig off to the barn or shed and lay it under a strong beam. A cammeril [like a hanger with notches] would be put through the pig's tendons, to hold the legs apart. The pig was hauled upside down so it was not touching the ground. Split the pig down the middle, take out innards, hold an apron round the pig to catch all the intestines; these were taken to a table and sorted out. Then split the pig straight down to the throat. The bladder, liver, heart and lights were all taken out.'

The bladder was used to store the lard, which could be kept this way for many months, although, if you were lucky, the bladder was

'Right where do I start?' Bernard and Colin Hutchinson of Ugthorpe tackling the piggy who stayed at home. (By kind permission of Sylvia Hutchinson)

dried and used as a football. The pig's fry of heart, liver and kidneys was put on a plate and sent round for the neighbours and the plate returned unwashed as it was considered bad luck to wash the plate and wash away a friendship.

> 'The pig was then left to hang there from Saturday, usually, until Monday. The backbone would then be split, the head cut off under the jaw and used for salting; snout and trotters went for brawn. The two lumps of fat under the ribs, "leaf fat", were rendered down for dripping or lard and what was left from rendering was called "scrappings" [now known as pork scratchings]. Some took out the ribs, others left them in and cut off the hams from the top of the ribs; then shaped ham in an oval shape, the cut off went for pork.'

Salting the pig was done with saltpetre pushed inside the skin and big blocks of salt crushed and rubbed onto and underneath the skin. Big pigs had to be left for three weeks and turned every two or three days with more salt rubbed in. Then the salt was rubbed off and the meat hung up to dry completely. Finally the sides and

Miss Thelma Jones, Rural Economy Domestic Instructor, demonstrating the art of bacon curing to a wartime Women's Institute audience in Ripon. (By kind permission of North Yorkshire West Federation of Women's Institutes)

hams were wrapped in muslin with a thin sack round them to keep off the flies.

Women were not afraid to get 'stuck in'. An old record book of the Ripon Group of Women's Institutes for December 1945 reported, 'A special group meeting was held in the Electricity Showroom, in the form of a lecture with slides on "The slaughtering of the pig and home curing of ham and bacon" by Miss Thelma Jones.' The lecture must have been good, as Miss Jones was back the next month demonstrating, 'Making the most of pig offal'.

If by now you have vowed never to eat pork again I will make amends by offering a very old Wensleydale recipe that is wonderful with roast pork:

Sugary Mustard

2 heaped teaspoons of made mustard
5 tablespoons of granulated sugar
4 tablespoons of double cream
1 tablespoon of vinegar

Mix all together and enjoy.

There is nothing finer than meat that has come free. Poaching rabbits went on, in spite of vigilant gamekeepers and landowners. Catching rabbits or breeding them was a good source of food and extra money.

> *'For rabbits young, and rabbits old,*
> *For rabbits hot and rabbits cold.*
> *For rabbits tender and rabbits tough,*
> *We thank thee Lord, we've had enough.'*

A Masham lady, as a young girl, regularly went with her farmer father to set rabbit snares in their fields. On the way to school she checked the snares and, if a rabbit was not dead, she killed it with the side of her hand, breaking the neck and then pressing the bladder to 'wee them out'. She hung the rabbits on the field gate and her mother collected them later to sell in the Masham shop.

'The Warrener', engraved by W. Ward and published by H. Morland, 1806. The warrener looked after fields enclosed with very high walls in which rabbits were bred for eating and there were large warrens throughout Yorkshire. When he made a sale he skinned the rabbit on the spot and kept the fur to sell on to the hat makers.

Game birds such as pheasant, partridge, grouse, wild duck, teal, snipe or woodcock seldom reached the tables of the working class, unless they were poached. A wartime cookery book advised supplementing the meat ration with roast sparrow, squirrel tail soup, hedgehog stew and pigeons. According to the recipe for Yorkshire pigeon pie, the meat is dry and needs a piece of fatty ham placed on the breast and some stock before enclosing in pastry and baking slowly for over an hour. Rooks were caught in large nets in the Dales and eaten during the second week in May, but again the meat cannot stand alone.

Rook Pie

Stew the breast meat gently with a small amount of beef steak and some beef dripping. When cool, remove bones and place in a pie dish with a little of the juices. Season with salt and cayenne pepper. Cover with shortcrust pastry and bake until pastry is brown.

Yorkshire men enjoyed their meat and did justice to whatever food was set before them, even if sometimes the amounts seemed excessive. The diary of the Reverend Benjamin Newton, the Vicar of Wath, near Ripon, recorded an entry for the 27th December 1817:

'Dined at Mr Allanson's. The party Mr and Mrs Walker, Mr Charnock, Miss and Miss A. Allanson, Captain Horn B.N., A.F.N., C.E.N. The most remarkable occurrence was Walker's eating. 1st a plate of haddock, 2nd a plate of fillet of veal and being twice helped to tongue, 3rd three slices of a saddle of mutton, 4th a large wing of a large duck, 5th two plates of roasting pig, 6th half the tail of a large lobster, 7th cheese and then desert. N.B. He had no wager on his eating...'

Perhaps he shared the philosophy of another yeoman farmer who declared, 'When I gans to anybody else's house I allus eats as mich as ever I can; coz if I'm welcome it pleases 'em; and if I isn't welcome it vexes 'em.'

FAT GOOSEBERRIES AND OTHER BEAUTIES

Gooseberry Fool

Cook gooseberries. While still hot stir in a little butter and sugar. When cold fold in an equal quantity of whipped cream.

There is nothing foolish about a gooseberry. Gooseberries are taken seriously in Yorkshire. Ray and I must have been a thundering nuisance when we visited the annual Egton Bridge Gooseberry Show at the beginning of August. This is a delightful event but not one taken lightly. We were treated with absolute courtesy by the members of the Egton Bridge Old Gooseberry Society as I took photographs and asked the sort of questions that showed my complete ignorance of the gooseberry.

Gooseberry clubs were popular in the late 18th and early 19th century in the industrial areas of the north of England. Many of the old gooseberry names, unknown today, reflected the Empire and past victories: 'Roaring Lion',

A major event in the world of gooseberry growing.

The weigh-in at the Egton Bridge Old Gooseberry Show.

'Nelson's Waves', 'Hero of the Nile' and 'Wellington's Glory' but 'Lord Kitchener', 'Admiral Beatty' and 'Lord Derby' grow on. The Egton Bridge Society was unusual because it was on the Yorkshire Moors, far away from any industry. In 1843 there were 148 gooseberry shows but today there is only the prestigious Egton Bridge show and some small shows in mid Cheshire.

Gooseberry growers come from far and wide bearing their entries in cottonwool-lined egg boxes. The secrets of growing champion gooseberries remain closely guarded, although I did learn that competitors shield the fruit with umbrellas when it rains, as a split in the skin would scupper any chance of winning. There are different classes with prizes and trophies for red, white, yellow and green gooseberries, but the heaviest of them all is the Champion Berry. The winner in 2005, a locally grown red berry called 'Lord Derby', weighed in at a hefty 28 drams 6 grains (27½ grains = 1 dram, and 16 drams = 1 ounce).

The gooseberry was once universally eaten, the tangy taste

refreshing to a manual worker on a hot day. A gooseberry bush was easy to grow, did not take up much room and could be sited anywhere. My friend Mary Alderson remembers as a child the path from the back door to the outside privy lined with gooseberry bushes, and very prickly they were, too, in the dark.

There was always a market for gooseberries: for jams, pies, wine, chutney and sauce to eat with fish. Those with a glut of gooseberries sold them from their garden, allotment or farm. In the 1800s many emigrated from north Yorkshire for a fresh start in the New World. One of these emigrants to America, Matthew Willis, wrote from Wisconsin to his nephew in 1849:

> 'Let the first of our friends that come over bring along with them Gooseberry seeds, if it is not too late to get them. Perhaps they will not be all done in the Yorescott garden. Let the berries be put in a small Box of dry sand, and bring along all together. I have never seen a garden Gooseberry since I came. If any good is to be done it is by raising such rarities as these.'

The Yorescott mentioned was a farm in Wensleydale. It is nothing new for farmers to look for other ways of making a living, and in the 1800s James Willis of Yorescott had already diversified. His income came from selling milk, cheese and butter from his dairy herd, ham, pork, bacon, beef, ducks and hens and their eggs, 'wine berries', rhubarb, gooseberries and herbs from his garden. Farmers had land to spare, but for others it was more difficult.

This is why the rise of the allotment was such a benefit to the working family. With the various Enclosure Acts from 1760 to 1820 common land was converted into private property, and land for ordinary people to cultivate vegetables and fruit, graze a goat and a few chickens was denied them. This meant moving to the towns for work, but in the 1800s life in the towns was crowded and unhealthy, and so waste land was 'allotted' to the working classes. One of the first to see the benefit of this was Titus Salt of Saltaire, who provided decent housing for his workers as well as allotments.

The Second World War and the 'Dig for Victory' campaign launched in 1939 saw every spare inch of back garden, allotment and park given over to the growing of vegetables. The famous Woolton Pie, named after the Minister for Food, consisted entirely of vegetables – potatoes, carrots, turnips and parsnips – in an oatmeal stock with a pastry crust.

What do Genghis Khan, Cleopatra, the Russian Tsars and Wakefield have in common? A love of rhubarb. Rhubarb is an ancient plant, first discovered in Siberia, and has benefited mankind for 3,000 years in medicine and as a highly nutritious food. During the Wakefield Festival of Rhubarb in February my research led me to the 18 square miles between Leeds, Wakefield and Bradford, known as the Yorkshire Rhubarb Triangle. The moisture-retaining soil here is ideal for rhubarb, with a high rainfall off the Pennines and nitrogen provided by 'shoddy', a waste product from the woollen industry. In the 1930s and 40s there were 200 growers and the rhubarb trains left nightly for London and Scotland. People ate huge amounts of rhubarb, without sugar, during the Second World War and a whole generation grew up hating it.

Rhubarb grown outside in the fields is ready from April but during the bleak months of January and February, strange and

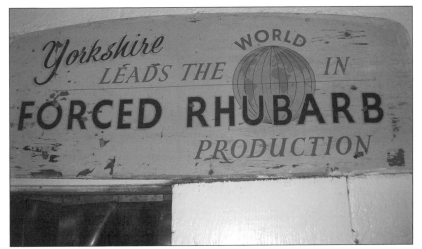

No arguing with this old sign at the forcing sheds of E. Oldroyds & Sons, Main Street, Carlton, Wakefield.

Rhubarb growing in the forcing sheds by candlelight in February. A tour not to be missed during the Wakefield Festival of Rhubarb – you can even hear the rhubarb growing. (By kind permission of Oldroyds of Carlton, Wakefield)

wonderful things happen in low, dark sheds. Between Christmas and New Year the rhubarb roots are lifted from outside and brought into the 'forcing sheds', where the tightly packed crowns are warmed, watered and lit by candlelight. The 'forced' rhubarb, with its lovely deep pink stems and curled yellow leaves, takes five to six weeks to grow this way, drawing sugar from its roots. It has a subtle sweet taste, ideal for balancing flavours in food with a high fat content. Rhubarb and crumble using 'forced rhubarb' is a queen among puddings and so in future, when I cook, I am not going to apologize that it is 'only rhubarb and crumble'.

'Never be humble about your crumble.'

Those readers who never eat anything that once had a face will have arrived at this chapter with relief, although, as a Victorian medical man once declared: 'Vegetarianism is harmless enough though apt to fill a man with wind and self righteousness'. In a country of meat-eaters there was a belief that certain vegetables would do you harm. Raw cucumber 'makes the churchyards prosperous'; aubergines were said to 'cause men to swerve from decent behaviour'; eating lettuce or onions made you tired; and the early Church disapproved of beans because they made the nuns 'unsettled', and the same went for cabbage when eaten by men!

Fortunately no such nonsense is attached to the potato, for without them no self-respecting Yorkshire man would consider a meal complete. 'When thoo hears t'cuckoo shout, it's tahme ti plant thi taties out.' This activity involved everyone, as the Carperby School Log Book of 1880 recorded: 'April – Irregular attendances at school, arriving late and leaving early. Some to dig their potato gardens, others to attend the sheep and lambs.' Many preferred an earlier date on Good Friday, as the earth then was thought good and holy and the early crop of potatoes would grow well.

Anyone who had a scrap of land cultivated beans. Even if it was just a backyard, or a flat roof, a large plant pot or a trough, everyone grew beans. Beans were believed to give energy and vitality, hence 'full of beans' and their 'windy' properties were all to the good.

> *Beans, beans, the musical fruit,*
> *The more you eat, the more you 'toot',*
> *The more you 'toot', the better you feel,*
> *So let's have beans for every meal.*

Real Yorkshire men were not afraid of eating a raw turnip. Farmers who felt 'peckish' out in the fields pulled a turnip, peeled it with a knife and ate it there and then. Others were not above pinching a turnip and enjoying it on the spot, although old men carried a spoon or a knife as their teeth were not up to the job. A turnip was thought to be a powerful aphrodisiac, and so there may have been a reason for a Yorkshire man's love of raw turnip.

A favourite on the east coast was cabbage. Fishermen on their weekly trip into Whitby for supplies carried a basket of herring on their head to sell but returned with a basket full of potatoes, bread and cabbage. They were fond of cabbage soup with a lump of meat in it. Yorkshire fishermen were introduced to the delights of cabbage by the Cornish fishermen who came to fish these waters and were fanatical cabbage-eaters. Until recently we preferred our cabbage limp and well cooked: boiled until it had surrendered, totally stripped of its vitamin A and C. Cabbage took a long time to cook, as the vicar found on asking his wife if lunch was nearly ready. She replied, 'Lunch will be ready in three quarters of an hour, my love. I've just put the cabbage on.'

For those who like cabbage, but not the lingering cooking smell, here is a tip from an old commonplace book, dated 1905 and written by a Bradford lady. 'The disagreeable smell produced by cabbage in the process of cooking may be got rid of if a piece of bread tied in a fine white rag is placed in the saucepan with the water. After this has been on the fire for quarter of an hour it should be taken out and thrown in the fire.'

To serve vegetables *al dente* in the past would have got the cook the sack. Vegetables were once cooked for much longer than is acceptable now but, in spite of this, they were not reduced to the watery, pulpy mess that you might imagine. The kitchen fire was lit most of the time; so the oven was hot, which suited the long, slow style of meat cooking needed to make cheap cuts tender. The vegetables were therefore added whole, not cut up, diced and generally fiddled with as we do today.

If there was a county dessert it had to be apple pie, eaten with cheese – 'an apple pie without the cheese is like a kiss without the squeeze' – even though Yorkshire is not known as an apple-growing county, unlike Kent and Worcestershire. Sadly the number of apples grown in this country has diminished, with 60% of supermarket apples imported, and we know who to blame for the tasteless, mushy apologies for apples we buy now. Anyone with an apple tree in the garden should cherish it.

The National Trust in Yorkshire has two orchards, at Beningbrough Hall and Nunnington Hall and, with their popular 'apple days' in October, are encouraging us to eat and cultivate local apples. Certain varieties do well in Yorkshire, those that flower late and ripen early. Apples need sunshine and well-drained

Brian Gable, a member of the Northern Fruit Group who helps with the fruit trees at Nunninton Hall, and a helper, David Hutchinson, producing apple juice from his cider press. Taken at an Apple Day event in October at Nunnington Hall near Helmsley. (By kind permission of The National Trust)

Gardening on the rooftops in the centre of Leeds. An old photograph from Ray's family, sadly there is no one left to tell us who these keen gardeners were, but the building was on Infirmary Street, just off City Square.

soil and apple growing once flourished in parts of Ryedale. 'Green Balsam' was once grown extensively in North Yorkshire and known as 'the farmer's wife's apple'. The famous dessert apple 'Ribston Pippin', sometimes called the 'Glory of York', has the highest vitamin C of any apple in cultivation and was raised at Ribston Hall near Knaresborough in 1709 from seeds brought from Normandy. 'Burr Knot' and 'Cockpit', both cookers from the East Riding, were first recorded in the early 1800s, and, even older, the 'Yorkshire Greening', a cooker from Pontefract, in 1769.

Growing in the orchard at Nunnington Hall is a lesser known Yorkshire cooking apple called 'Dog's Snout', which, I am told, is nicer than it sounds. At the Apple Day I heard the story of a rare apple from Doncaster called 'Syke House', locally pronounced 'sick house'. When the apple was exported to Holland, its name was translated by the Dutch as *ziekenhuis appel* 'hospital apple'.

First prize at the Askrigg Produce Show 2005 for Annie Bennett with her collection of vegetables. The Askrigg Show, like so many, was started as a response to the 'Dig for Victory' campaign. Other shows may have folded but this one is as popular as ever. (Photograph by Kate Empsall)

The grand country houses in Yorkshire compensated for the cold by having heated glasshouses for forcing fruit, vegetables and flowers. The walled kitchen gardens, well out of view of the big house, had hollow walls with flues running through them with a fire lit at one end to heat the wall. Thus a Yorkshire gentleman could look forward to his own home-grown peaches, but those with an ordinary vegetable patch had to use other ways. On the east coast tomatoes did well, helped perhaps by a special local fertilizer. Soot, lime, horse *mig* (a local word for urine) and one-year-old hen droppings were all stirred in a tank of cold water and this stinking liquid worked into the soil. I have always enjoyed a tomato up until now!

> *'Knowledge is knowing a tomato is a fruit,*
> *Wisdom is not putting it into a fruit salad.'*

YORKSHIRE DELICACIES PAST AND PRESENT

'A pork pie, a half pint, a cigarette, a box of matches – and you'll still get change from sixpence'.

1930s' advertisement
Arthur Cowling's West Riding Wine Lodges

Yorkshire pies and Proust – not an obvious connection, but the smell of madeleines transported Proust back to his childhood and for many so too does the smell of a hot pork pie. The pies of a Yorkshire childhood marked the special days: a fine 'standing' pork pie placed proudly on the table for Boxing Day tea; a Saturday morning trip to the market pie stall for a solid meat pie, mushy peas with mint sauce or a *trunnel* pie of hot chopped tripe with peas on top. Meat pies in Ray's childhood were known as 'growlers', but we will not delve further into the reasons for this name.

Never trust a Yorkshire man when it comes to a meat pie. Two men were on a train returning home to Lancashire when the train stopped at Skipton. One of the men opened the window and asked a young lad lounging nearby if he would get them two meat pies and one for himself for his trouble and handed him the money. The lad rushed back after a couple of minutes stuffing a pie into his mouth. The man demanded, 'Where's mi meat pies?' 'Here's your change mister,' said the lad. 'They onny 'ad one left.'

It goes without saying that in Yorkshire there was probably the biggest feast ever: it is the stuff of legends. In January 1466 the dukes of Gloucester and Suffolk, two earls, three bishops and thirty-one heads of religious houses visited Cawood Castle, south of York. It was said that 6,000 guests sat down to dine and 1,000 cooks worked in 500 kitchens preparing among other things: '104 oxen, 6 wylde bulls, 1,000 muttons, 304 veales, 304 porkes, 400 swannes, 2,000 geese, 104 peacocks, 2,000 pyges, 400 plovers, 100 curlews, stagges, bucks, porpoises and seales ...' The list went on, plus puddings of: 7,000 cold baked custards and tartes, spices, sugared delicacies and wafers – plenty.'

Nearly 600 years on and the Archbishop of York can still throw a party. Some 3,500 people filled York Minster when Dr John Sentamu was enthroned as the ninety-seventh Archbishop of York on 30th November 2005. The lively service combined Anglican liturgy and African drums, singers and dancers, with the vegetarian wrap, flap jack, and fruit, supplied by Marks and Spencer. I suppose it was too much to expect oxen and wild bulls.

York Mayne Bread 'hath been used in this City time out of mind of man ...' and was presented to distinguished visitors.

York Mayne Bread

12 ozs plain flour
8 ozs sugar
a good teaspoon each of coriander and
carraway seeds.
2 teaspoons rose water.
3 egg yolks and 2 egg whites.
½ oz yeast
⅓ cup warm milk and water

Mix together the flour, sugar and seeds. In a basin add the rose water to the 3 egg yolks. In another basin beat the egg whites until stiff, and in a third basin mix the yeast, warm water and milk.

Mix the contents of the three basins with the dry ingredients and put to rise in a warm place for approximately 20 minutes. Roll out the dough, cut into shape, and allow it to rise again for 10 minutes. Bake in a moderate oven for 10 minutes or until golden brown.

By the end of the 1500s spice cake, with ginger, was more popular, probably because it tasted better. The combination of carraway seeds, coriander and rose water is not one that immediately appeals. York City Corporation was dismayed that this unique bread was no longer made and in 1595 passed a motion that the city bakers must bake 'every Friday morning 10 shillings worth of Mayne bread at least, to be sold to such as will buy it'. If the bread did not sell by late afternoon, the lord mayor, aldermen and sheriffs had to buy it. What they did with all this stale bread is not known; perhaps it went to the poor. The baking and selling of spice cakes was prohibited with a hefty fine of 40 shillings, but it was a losing battle and, by 1622, York Mayne bread had disappeared.

Another historical dish was the Stamford Bridge Spear or Pear Pie. In 1066 a great battle, the last Saxon victory in England, took place at Stamford Bridge between the English, led by King Harold, and the invading Norwegians. The English tried to cross the river at the old wooden bridge but were held back by an intrepid Norseman who defied all comers. A resourceful Englishman sailed underneath the bridge and thrust upwards with his spear (shades of Corporal Jones in *Dad's Army*) through the holes in the bridge and quickly despatched the fellow, thus opening the bridge for the English. Harold and his exhausted men then marched back down south to fight the Battle of Hastings, and the rest, as they say, is history.

Spear or pear pies were once made and sold at the Stamford Bridge Feast in September to mark this grim episode but the exact recipe is lost. The pies were apparently pastry boats about four inches long and filled with spiced Hazel pears with the stalk left in place to represent the spear; other versions have a metal meat skewer placed upright in the pastry boat. It seems likely that, just as with mince pies, the original pies were made with meat rather than anything sweet.

The York ham has stood the test of time. A proper York ham should be dry cured, dark cream on the outside with pale pink meat. In less

hygienic times it was kept in a linen bag to keep the flies off and hung in a cool dark pantry. There is a story of the original hams being smoked with oak sawdust left over from the building of York Minster, but who knows. Farms in the Vale of Pickering and the Wolds were centres for Large White pigs, but other farms and dairies kept pigs to eat the whey run off during cheese making. Small breweries supplied the local pigs with used brewers grain which, together with good quality salt for curing the meat, made for a very special taste. One of life's sublime eating experiences is ham and eggs after a good walk in the Yorkshire countryside.

Yorkshire boasts the biggest picnics, parties and pies. Has there ever been a bigger pie than the Denby Dale Bicentenary Pie, revealed on the 3rd of September 1988 to an estimated crowd of 100,000 people? It contained 6,600 lbs of beef, 6,600 lbs of potatoes and 1,500 lbs of onions; and Ray and I were there – but we never got near enough to have a slice.

There is something touching about the first pie baked by the villagers of Denby Dale in 1788 to celebrate George III's return to

The Infirmary Pie of 1928. A new oblong dish measuring 16 feet by 5 feet replaced the old circular one. Eighteen ladies and five butchers prepared four bullocks and 600 lbs of potatoes.

sanity. They cooked again in 1815, producing a Victory Pie for the Duke of Wellington's victory over Napoleon. The Corn Law Act of 1815 had protected the interests of the landed gentry, allowing inflated prices for their corn. The poor rejoiced when the repeal of the law meant they could once again afford bread and, in 1846, Denby Dale celebrated with a circular pie measuring seven feet in diameter and two feet deep with generous amounts of mutton, beef, hare, rabbit, partridge, pheasant, fowl, pigeon and 63 small birds. The pie proved too heavy for its stage, which collapsed, the pie spilling out and being eaten by the villagers in 'riotous circumstances'. There was an ugly rumour of sabotage, as the nearby village of Clayton West had already made an enormous celebratory plum pie and were not about to be upstaged.

The pie to celebrate Queen Victoria's Golden Jubilee in 1887 contained meat, game and poultry in an even larger pie dish. The cooking was overseen by a London chef, who, when he realized all was not well, hastily left, leaving a pie that overwhelmed the crowd of 15,000 with its noxious smell. The pie had a hasty burial under large quantities of quick lime in a local wood. Not to be beaten by this disaster, the village women made the Resurrection Pie a week

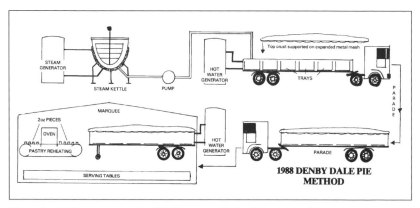

How to cook a giant pie. Environmental health regulations meant a more sophisticated system for cooking the pie. The pie filling of beef, potatoes, onions and gravy was cooked in steam kettles in ¼ ton batches and put into 12 trays contained in a much larger tray with hot water circulating. The puff pastry pie crust was supported on six sections of metal mesh.

Mass catering: Bainbridge Women's Institute Christmas supper party, January 1955. (Ann Holubecki Collection)

later, making a note never to include game again in the pie nor to let an outsider meddle with it.

The pie of 1896 for the 50th anniversary of the repeal of the Corn Laws was a success. However, the 1928 Infirmary Pie, which raised £1,000 to endow a bed at the Huddersfield Royal Infirmary, stuck in the oven until twenty local men with crowbars manoeuvred it out with the help of steel tram rails. A poetical souvenir by Brisco Brayton proclaimed:

> *Why to-day to Denby Dale do thousands of people hie?*
> *To see a sight that ne'er again may please the human eye.*
> *It is the largest Pie, that the world has ever seen;*
> *And has been cooked at Denby Dale amid the fields so green.*
> *The Pie is fourteen yards all round. All Denby's made its crust.*
> *Its meat and taties weigh three ton (these figures you can trust).*
> *Five bullocks rest inside the Pie, along with other meat;*
> *The gravy measures gallons; and 'by gum it is a treat'.*

There have been three further pies: in 1964 money was raised for a new village hall, and 30,000 people tucked into a pie containing three tons of beef; the Bicentenary Pie in 1988; and another in 2000, as part of the Millennium celebrations. This last one was blessed by the Bishop of Wakefield, and the great Yorkshireman, former cricket umpire Dickie Bird, cut the first slice.

There have been and still are some great independent Yorkshire butchers making proper pork pies, black puddings and sausages. Albert Hirst was a fine example of the old-fashioned butcher. He established his business at 25 Cheapside Barnsley in 1897 and was famous for his pork pies and medal-winning black puddings – 'the caviar of the north', as he called it. Letters reached him from all over the world even when simply addressed to 'The Black Pudding King, England', but he was also responsible for bringing the Barnsley chop to a wider audience.

In the mid 19th century farmers at Barnsley Market enjoyed a midday meal of the special mutton chop served at the King's Head

Albert and John Hirst, sons of Albert Hirst, preparing 75 Barnsley chops for the opening of Barnsley Town Hall in December 1933. (By kind permission of the Archives & Local Studies Department, Barnsley Metropolitan Borough Council)

Hotel in Market Hill. A stranger who had heard of this dish called at the hotel and asked for 'one of your big chops – a real chop. You know, a Barnsley chop'. Thus the majestic chop was named.

A Barnsley chop then was like a small roast: a thick mutton chop, three ribs thick, from the tender middle of the loin, and weighing between ¾ lb and 1½ lbs. It took a whole sheep to produce just two of these splendid chops, one from each side of the backbone, but over the years it appears to have become something different. When I asked a number of people, including some butchers, for their definition of a Barnsley chop, all said it was two generous size chops, still attached and spread like a butterfly, from either side of the sheep's backbone. Personally, I am going for the Albert Hirst option. Ideally the chops were hung for two weeks to enrich the flavour, and then were either dipped in boiling fat to seal them and cooked for 40 minutes in a hot oven, or, if unsealed, roasted for 75 minutes. The traditional accompaniments were warm potato crisps and Barnsley Bitter.

The late Duke of Windsor, when he was Prince of Wales, opened Barnsley Town Hall in December 1933 and 75 Barnsley chops were served at the celebratory lunch. What must the Duke have thought when faced with such a generous portion – I have always thought he looked a bit on the puny side – and did he manage to eat it?

If there is confusion over the exact nature of a Barnsley chop in Yorkshire, imagine the mystery to those outside the county. The *Barnsley Town Hall Civic Review* published a letter received years later from a Devonshire man:

> 'Zur, Can y plaize tell oi wot be a 'Barnsley Chop'? Oih 'ere yeard tell o' un. Us be chaps wot aits Demsher Dumplins an' crame an drinks gude rough Demsher Zider. Your bit o' mutton sounds alright, if us uses Dartmoor sheep instead, 'cause us too be gude Trenchermen. Yours respectful loike.'

It is a proud boast that West Riding fish and chips, cooked in beef dripping, are the best in the world. In search of the authentic taste when he lived in the south, Ray drove miles to the only fish and chip shop he knew that was owned by a Yorkshireman. Who first put fried fish and chips together is a food mystery, but it was probably Jewish immigrants in London. Charles Dickens wrote of a 'fried fish warehouse' in *Oliver Twist* in 1839, and hot potatoes were sold by street traders everywhere. The oldest shop selling fish, dipped in a batter of flour and water, together with chips, belonged to a Jewish immigrant Joseph Malin in the early 1860s in London. However, in the north around that time, 'Granny' Duce owned several combined greengrocers and fish and chip shops in Bradford, and in Lancashire chipped potatoes were on sale in Oldham, but without the fish.

Fish and chips were a popular, cheap meal, and there were fish and chip shops on practically every street corner of industrial West Yorkshire. In the 1920s and 30s, mill workers sent out for bulk orders of fish and chips for their midday meal. Friday was the day for a take-home teatime or supper treat: a 'penn'orth' of chips plus haddock or cod costing 2d or 3d, or a fish cake at 1½d. If you wanted to eat in a fish and chip café you had fish and chips with bread, butter and a pot of tea for 9d, but, if all this was beyond your means, there was always 'a ha'porth of scraps', the bits of batter that came off in the frying.

The sign of a first-class fish and chip shop, often with a café, is a lengthy queue outside. A name synonymous with fish and chips is the legendary Harry Ramsden, now a global name, with fish and chip restaurants across the world. He was a visionary businessman, who created the world's largest fish and chip shop with restaurant and was devoted to the quality of his food. It was in his blood, as his father had a fish and chip shop in Bradford in the 1900s, but Harry looked elsewhere and in 1928 bought a wooden shed measuring ten feet by six feet in Otley Road, White Cross, Guiseley. From here he sold his fish and chips and by 1931 he had opened his restaurant. Everything was of the highest quality, with fitted carpets, chandeliers, leaded-light windows and monogrammed cutlery, which sadly 'disappeared' as his customers took home a souvenir. The splendid surroundings led one little boy to ask, 'Dad, is this where God comes for his fish and chips?'

Liquorice, also known as Spanish juice, is a Mediterranean plant. How it arrived in Pontefract is the stuff of legends, but most likely,

Pontefract or Pomfret cakes, once known as Yorkshire Pennies. One is never enough.

as with so many things, it was the monks in the late 12th century who introduced it. The soil around Pontefract proved ideal for the liquorice plant, and the citizens guarded their special crop with zeal. A town meeting in 1701 forbad anyone to give, sell or lend any liquorice buds or setts for growing outside the borough. The original Pontefract or Pomfret cake was a medicine for coughs and colds, and also an efficient laxative, but in 1760 a local apothecary, George Dunhill, added sugar and started making liquorice sweets. By 1900 there were fifteen manufacturers of Pontefract cakes in the town. During the Second World War, when sweets were rationed, children bought liquorice roots from the chemist and chewed them instead. Liquorice growing declined from then onwards but the cakes are still made, now using imported extract.

Yorkshire has a fine tradition of confectionery. In the 1700s York had several family businesses devoted to the importing of citrus peel and the manufacture of lozenges and confits made from nuts, seeds and sugar.

Always a Top Ten favourite according to the confectioners, Chocolatiers of Ripon.

Joseph Terry from Pocklington served an apprenticeship in York as an apothecary and set up in business in 1815. By 1830 he was not only dealing in sugar-coated pills and potions but also in bakery and sweets. Thomas Craven left Acklam near Malton in 1833 for an apprenticeship in the York confectionery trade. The company he founded was responsible in 1900 for introducing the sugared almond from France. Joseph Rowntree, the son of a York grocer, together with his younger brother Henry, began manufacturing chocolates and other sweets in York from 1869. His Quaker beliefs meant he was an enlightened employer and concerned with social reform to improve the conditions of the poor. Countless children since then will also thank him for the introduction in 1881 of the fruit pastille, followed by chocolate drops, fruit gums and, best of all, jelly babies.

However, York did not have a monopoly on the sweet industry, as John Mackintosh (born 1868) was the owner of a small shop in Halifax and founded a large confectionery empire on the strength of Mrs Mackintosh's excellent toffee. Their Quality Street brand, with the distinctive picture of a soldier and lady, was inspired by a 1901 stage play of the same name, which featured these two characters; it was written by J. M. Barrie, better known for *Peter Pan*.

Farrah's Original Harrogate Toffee, a cross between butterscotch and barley sugar, is still being made by hand in an open copper pan, 28 lbs at a time. The company was founded in 1840 by a baker, John Farrar, using his mother's recipe. Her toffee was designed to clear the mouth of the awful taste of the Harrogate sulphur waters. The original shop was straight across the road from the Pump Room and, as you had to drink two pints of the water in one go to do any good, you can imagine the gentry reeling out of the Pump Room in search of something sweet to take away the taste.

From the lush pastures of Coverdale, Ribblesdale and Swaledale comes milk to make excellent cheese but, as I live in Wensleydale, I shall stick to what I know. The mild, creamy white, crumbly Wensleydale cheese is perfect for eating with a tangy sweet apple pie or a full bodied fruit cake. The cheese has a long history and many devotees. J Alderson wrote passionately of its qualities in his poem 'To A Wensleydale Cheese':

> *'A'll stick up fer the' wharivver Ah be,*
> *It's flavour et coonts wi' a fella like me.*
> *Thoo's bin a favourite a' mine sin Ah wer a lad,*
> *Thoo's t' best cheese i' t'wo'ld!*
> *Thoo's best et Ah've 'ad.'*

The first Wensleydale cheese from ewes milk must have been a tedious business, milking sheep twice a day. It was made by Cistercian monks, who first attempted farming at Fors Abbey near Askrigg, but their crops failed, the natives were hostile, and they were troubled by wolves. They retreated to a more gentle site at Jervaulx in 1156 to continue as sheep farmers and horse breeders. The secret of making a good cheese was passed on at the dissolution of the monasteries to a local family, and it was about this time the cow took its proper place.

For centuries wives toiled away making cheese during the summer months when the cows were in the fields and the milk

Making cheese the old way. Milk out of a back can (the container used when milking cows in the fields) was poured through a sieve into a copper cheese kettle. The kettle was hung in front of the fire to raise the temperature of the milk to 85°F, then rennet was added and the milk left to stand until it had curdled.   (Ann Holubecki Collection)

A curd-breaker (like a table tennis bat with wires) cut the curds, which were then hung in a muslin cloth to strain off the whey for four hours. The curds were then crumbled, salt added, and then packed into a cheese vat lined with muslin, with the sinker lid on top. (Ann Holubecki Collection)

A collection of wooden cheese vats with iron hoops. A cast-iron cheese press is in the foreground. The cheese vat was left in the cheese press overnight and then the cheese taken out and bandaged with calico. It was then stored in the cheese room, and turned twice daily at first, and then once a day. (Ann Holubecki Collection)

The popular shop at the Wensleydale Creamery, Hawes, where you can taste before buying.

yield was high. The cheeses were generally 4 to 5 lbs in weight, but the quality varied depending on the local grass, the health of the cow and whether the woman making the cheese had 'cheese hands'. It was women's work, although an old superstition believed that no menstruating woman should ever go in the dairy to make butter or cheese or everything would go 'off'.

Farmhouse Wensleydale cheese was bought by factors, who sold it on in the towns or at autumn fairs, but there were several renowned women cheese-makers who dealt directly with their customers. One family in Carperby supplied Fortnum and Mason in the late 1800s and Mary Scarr of Colby Hall had a very exclusive client list. Her grandson James Scarr still farms and supplies milk for cheese, just yards from where the monks made cheese centuries ago, at the long disappeared Fors Abbey. With her 'cheese hands', Mary Scarr's handmade farmhouse Wensleydale cheeses were in demand from the highest in the land. At night she sat at the kitchen table wrapping her cheeses in brown paper and string ready to be sent off to London and elsewhere on the train.

Not everyone was so skilled, and the farmhouse cheeses were hit and miss in their quality. In 1897 a local corn and provision merchant Edward Chapman decided to buy the milk from the farmers and make more quality-assured cheese in a cheese factory converted from a local woollen mill between Gayle and Hawes. The renowned Dalesman, Kit Calvert, continued its development and the successful Wensleydale Creamery still continues a proud tradition of cheese-making to this day.

A useful booklet *Good Things Made, Said and Done for Every Home and Household*, published in Leeds in 1884 promised, 'In the foregoing pages, the female head of a family who wishes to keep a good table according to her circumstances cannot fail to find a large number of valuable recipes as to what to cook, and how to cook it'. Most of the recipes carried the additional information, 'this will be greatly improved by the addition of Yorkshire Relish the capital sauce manufactured by Messrs. Goodall, Backhouse & Co'.

Originally, Yorkshire relish was a good 'livener' for Yorkshire pudding, cold meat and salad. Yorkshire housewives had their own version of the piquant sauce made from black treacle, onions, brown sugar and spiced vinegar. It was first made commercially in Leeds in 1837. Robert Goodall, a chemist (another apothecary/ chemist connection with food), used his wife's recipe. In addition to improving quotations such as 'Eat in measure and defy the doctor', the book gave the 'good housewife' weekly menus for those who were comfortably off, featuring roast beef, goose, veal and jugged hare. The weekly menus 'suitable for artisans' consisted of mutton in all its forms with – yes, you've guessed it – Yorkshire relish.

The *Oxford English Dictionary* gives the definition of relish as, among other things. '1. Flavour, distinctive taste, dash or tinge of some quality; appetizing flavour, attractive quality, enjoyment of food or other things, liking for, zest, thing eaten with plainer food to add flavour. 2. Serve as relish, to make piquant etc; get pleasure out of, be pleased with.' I hope you have found some of these qualities in this book on Yorkshire food and drink and that you are left, as you close the book, feeling satisfied and full with no sign of indigestion. So, to end with a final word from the past on hearty eating in Yorkshire:

'Remember it's your stomach that 'ods your back up.'

AND FINALLY – YOCKEN

'Look 'e here, look 'e there, look all over the table,
Let every man tak' up his spade, and eat whate'er he's able.'

arval bread	once eaten at funerals in the Keighley area. Funerals became known as 'arvills'
bait	worker's packed lunch
barm	yeast
barm cake	a type of bread bun with currants and raisins
brandy snaps	once a speciality of the ancient Hull fair
brewis or browis	an oatcake softened with hot water, then spread with animal fat or butter and seasoned with salt and pepper. Water brewis was without the fat or butter
brigg-shot	simple cold roast beef, once supplied free to drinkers by certain pubs in Leeds in order to keep their custom
cat-lap	weak tea
clap cake	a kind of oatcake made by throwing the mixture onto a board ('to clap' means to do something quickly)
crappins	pig fat, cooked and eaten. Also scrappings, scratchings
crowdy	oatmeal and water flavoured with salt or treacle
dog-'eeards	lumps in the porridge
drinkings	food and drink eaten in the fields by the workers
fat rascals	a cake with currants and sultanas, larger than a scone. When made on the north Yorkshire moors, they were cooked over

	an open turf or peat fire which gave a smoky flavour. Other names for similar types of cake were turf, warm, turn, sod and backstone
fish 'oil	fish and chip shop. Also chip 'oil
fuddle	a party or get together with food, especially at Christmas
Gayle 'watter' bannock	currants and sugar mixed together with a little water and placed in the centre of any dough left over after bread-making. The sides were folded together, rolled again, and baked
grunter	in east-coast fishing communities, another word for a pig. To say the word 'pig', especially while baiting the lines, was thought unlucky
jock	workman's food
midgerum fat	fat stripped from round a pig's bowels
minnin'-on	a snack
mint pasty	originally a Leeds pastry, made by sprinkling currants and chopped mint on one half of a round of shortcrust pastry and then topping with sugar and dabs of butter; with the pastry folded over and the edge crimped, it is baked in a hot oven until crisp
moggy	a basic dough mixture but with golden syrup
nappie ale	strong ale
oven bottom cake	a bread bun made with dough left over from bread making, rolled and spread with lard, kneaded again, rolled out to 1 inch thickness, and then baked in a hot oven; eaten split and buttered
parpin	salt
pickle, piddle	to play with your food
pogged	full
reasty bacon	bacon that is going off or rancid
	An old cure was a suppository made from the fat of rancid bacon.

sad cake	a cake cooked at the bottom of the oven and unlikely to rise, as it was made with plain flour, bacon fat, salt and water
saim	dripping
scaldings	unshelled peas boiled in the pod and dipped into melted butter seasoned with pepper, salt and vinegar and then drawn through the teeth to extract the peas
scallion	a spring onion
scone	(in Keighley) a fish cake
snap	a workman's packed lunch
spice	sweets
stingo	(mainly South Yorkshire) strong beer from the first brewing
swimmer	(West Riding) a locally made pork pie served with hot mushy peas, salt, pepper and vinegar
swizzle	drink
whanghy cheese	a type of cheese made from skimmed milk; the lack of fat makes it hard and dry, and suitable only for cooking
yocken	to eat and drink with pleasure

ACKNOWLEDGEMENTS

I have received much generous help with this book, and grateful thanks must go in particular to the following people:

Ann Holubecki, for allowing me unlimited use of the papers, books and photographs from her collection
Anne Bell, Eleanor Dinsdale and Margaret Knowles, for advice on baking and recipes
Colin Gray of the Egton Bridge Old Gooseberry Society
Sylvia Hutchinson, Tom Roe and Ron Stephenson of the Whitby Archives and Heritage Centre, Flowergate, Whitby, for their unstinting help with all matters relating to fishing and pigs
Marie-Hélène Milner, for her translation of Lady Bolton's menus
Marion Moverley, for sharing her research on Yorkshire funerals
Brian Gable, for his advice on the apples at Nunnington Hall.

Evelyn Abraham, Sid Barnett, Elizabeth Bradley, Daphne Clarke, Yvonne Coupé, Kate Empsall, Harold Hammond, Marie Hartley, Richard Fawcett, Josephine Hopper, Marian Kirby, Dulcea Kneeshaw, Brian Morland, Jean Moore, Eleanor Scarr, Edna Stanley and Sylvia Turner, for information and pictures.

The Sutcliffe Gallery, 1 Flowergate, Whitby, for the use of two photographs by Frank Meadow Sutcliffe Hon. F.R.P.S. (1853-1941), copyright The Sutcliffe Gallery, by agreement with Whitby Literary and Philosophical Society. For further information on their prints visit www.sutcliffe-gallery.co.uk or 01947 602239.

Bettys and Taylors of Harrogate

The archivists, librarians and all those who were so patient with my enquiries, especially:
The Archives and Local Studies Department, Barnsley Metropolitan Council
The Local Studies Department, Central Library, Department of Arts, Heritage and Leisure, City of Bradford Metropolitan District Council

The Brontë Society, Brontë Parsonage Museum, Haworth, Keighley
The Special Collections, Brotherton Library, Leeds University
The Dales Countryside Museum, Hawes
The National Trust, East Riddlesden Hall, Keighley
The National Trust, Nunnington Hall, Nunnington
John Goodchild of the John Goodchild Collection, Wakefield
The Lawrence Sterne Trust, Shandy Hall, Coxwold
Whitby Museum and Art Gallery, Pannett Park, Whitby
York Castle Museum
York City Archives
York Minster Library and Archives.

Finally, my husband Ray who helped in so many ways and, while I was away from the kitchen writing this book, became a tolerably good cook.

BIBLIOGRAPHY

The Bolton Castle Book of Recipes by Anne the Stillroom Maid, 1951

The Carperby School Log Books extracts from 1877–1915, held at Northallerton County Record Office

Cassell's County Cookbook – Yorkshire, Carol Wright, 1975

A Dales Countryside Cookbook, compiled by Janet Rawlings, 1993

Dales Memories, Marie Hartley and Joan Ingilby, 1986

Days of Yore – A History of Masham, Susan Cunliffe-Lister

The 1988 Denby Dale Bicentenary Pie Souvenir Brochure – A slice of History, Sheila Fewster

Eating With The Victorians, edited by C. Anne Wilson, 2004

English Housewifery, Elizabeth Moxon, 1775

The Essential West Riding, Herbert Whone, 1975

Food in England, Dorothy Hartley, 1954

Harry Ramsden – The Uncrowned King of Fish and Chips, Don Mosey & Harry Ramsden Junior, 1989

Making Cheese & Butter, Marie Hartley & Joan Ingilby, 1997

Making Oatcake, Marie Hartley & Joan Ingilby, 1998

North Yorkshire Within Living Memory, compiled by the North Yorkshire Federations of Women's Institutes, 1995

The Old Coaching Days in Yorkshire, T Bradley, 1889

Old Inns & Taverns of Yorkshire, Frank Graham, 1965

Progress in Pudsey, Joseph Lawson, 1887

Scarborough and the Yorkshire Coast, Ward Lock & Co, 1939

The Yorkshire Way, compiled by members of Yorkshire Federation of Women's Institutes, 1979

Traditional Food in Yorkshire, Peter Brears, 1987

Wensleydale Cheese, Kit Calvert, 1977

York, John Harvey, 1975

York History, number 2 issued by York Educational Settlement, edited by A J Peacock

The Yorkshire Anthology, collected by James O Halliwell, 1851

The Yorkshire Dictionary of Dialect, Tradition and Folklore, Arnold Kellett, 1994

Yorkshire Wit, Character, Folklore and Customs, Richard Blakeborough, 1898